TUNES

FROM

THE

TUG

AND OTHERS

Coach F. Glen Smith

GLEN SMITH
1905 Washington Avenue
Saint Albans, WV 25177-3128

International Standard Book Number 0-87012-740-3
Library of Congress Control Number 2005907724
Printed in the United States of America
Copyright © 2005 by Franklin G. Smith
St. Albans, WV
All Rights Reserved
2005

Printed by
McClain Printing Company
Parsons, WV 26287
www.mcclainprinting.com
2005

DEDICATION

This collection of poetry is dedicated to all the wonderful people of my hometown of Kermit, especially my Grandmother, Leotie Patrick, who taught me about living. I loved her very much. To my parents, Walter and Nellie Smith, to my brothers, Harry and Jack, and to all my Aunts and Uncles and my relatives. A special thanks to my wife, Shelby, for putting up with me for 45 years. Thanks to my daughters, Jeanie and Renee, and my sons-in-law, Rande and Tommy. To my Grandchildren, Rainer and Rachael, that have made my days more enjoyable. I'd like to thank all my doctors that saved my life many years ago and are doing so today. Furthermore, I would like to dedicate this book to all my teachers, especially Ruby Meade Robinson, Coach Virgil Hoke, and Amanda Meade Brewer—they were an inspiration to me and did those little extra things. Lastly, to the Tug River and the wonderful Town of Kermit that left me with some beautiful memories, tales, stories, and jokes that I have for many years tried to write. I call this collection of poems:

TUNES FROM THE TUG

ABOUT THE AUTHOR

Glen Smith was born in Warfield, Kentucky in 1933. His parents were Walter Smith and Nellie Patrick. He was raised by his Grandmother Leotie Patrick after his mother died of tuberculosis. He lived in Kermit, West Virginia and graduated from Kermit High School in May of 1950. He spent most of his youth in the Tug Valley in Mingo County.

In 1950, he went to Concord College on a basketball scholarship. There he played point guard for them and graduated in 1954. He did Master's Degree work at the University of Georgia and George Peabody College of Nashville, Tennessee. He was a school teacher and coached for 34 years in West Virginia including Kermit High School in Mingo County and Spring Hill Junior High School and McKinley Junior High School in Kanawha County. He taught Science, Social Studies, Health, and Physical Education at those schools.

He retired from teaching in 1988 and currently lives in St. Albans, West Virginia where he continues to write. At the present time, he has written more than 70 short stories and a novel to his credit. After his "TUNES FROM THE TUG" is published, he hopes to have other books to follow.

Mr. Smith's poems reflect the unique role that the Tug River ("Tug Fork of the Big Sandy") has played in the history of our country, and the role that the Tug River Valley had in shaping the lives and memories of Mr. Smith. The Tug River valley was long used by Indians as a highway to travel between the New River Valley in Virginia and the Ohio. The Virginia Militia also used the Tug River route to attack Indians in Ohio, as attested to by a roadside sign at the entrance to Mr. Smith's hometown of Kermit. That sign informs that it is the site of a Camp of Major (later General) Andrew Lewis in 1756 with Virginia troops, led by Smith, Hogg, Preston and others on way to attack Indians in Ohio. Members of that and other expeditions, together with friends and relatives, made up an important component of the early settlers of the Tug and Big Sandy River valleys. Many of the descendents of those early settlers remained in Valley throughout Mr. Smith's childhood. Those early settlers and their descendents formed bonds that lasted through generations. Smith and Preston, for instance, were part of that 1756 expedition and the Smith and Preston families were prominent in Kermit in Mr. Smith's childhood.

The Tug River Valley contains the Pocahontas coalfield, one of the nation's most valuable. The Norfolk and Western ("N&W") Railroad constructed a railway along the Tug River to haul coal from the many mines that were opened in the early 1900's. Many small communities, including Kermit and Matewan (of "The Matewan Massacre" fame) sprung up along the Tug River to house coal miners and the infrastructure to serve them. Many of Kermit's residents, including Mr. Smith's father, were coal miners who had to endure hardships, including working under "Yellow Dog" contracts, in order to feed their families.

Mingo County, and the communities along the Tug, became a bloody battle ground during the first half of the 20th century as the miners sought the right to join a union, the United Mine Workers ("UMW"), to engage in collective bargaining with the mine operators for higher pay and improvements in safety measures in the mines. Much of the conflict occurred upon the Operator's use of blacks from the south and emigrates from Europe to replace striking miners. The miners turned to violence to try to protect their jobs and the Operators hired what they called detective agencies, such as Baldwin Felts detective agency, to keep their mines operating.

Events that occurred during those mine wars, including the Matewan Massacre, Martial Law in Mingo County, the murder of Sid Hatfield, the Battle of Blair Mountain, the "Yellow Dog Contracts," and the treason trials, received national attention and played a prominent role in the passage of the National Industrial Recovery Act legislation.

Open warfare essentially ended in 1933, shortly after Mr. Smith's birth, with President Roosevelt's New Deal legislation (including the National Industrial Recovery Act) giving labor the statutory right to engage in collective bargaining. But several serious strikes occurred after such legislation, as the union negotiated with the coal Operators for better pay and safer working conditions. Violence broke out during those strikes when miners acted to close small mines that did not use union labor.

Mr. Smith and his friends grew up under the strain of the tension between miners and mine operators, and that tension had an impact on the quality of their lives. They also lived with the strain of having a father or brothers working in underground mines during a time when fatal and crippling mine accidents were commonplace.

TABLE OF CONTENTS

FORWARD

I am a former teacher, having taught forty-eight years. Glen Smith and his two brothers, were students of mine. Parents, in that time, were generally interested in what their children were learning.

It was obvious that Glen was multi-talented. He wrote poetry, prose and did some illustrating. I have many of his works and encouraged him, as with all of my students, to be proud of their talents and capabilities.

The Smith boy's mother passed away at an early age, which was a terrible blow, not only to them, but also to all in our small town. Grandmother Patrick asked the boys' father to move in to her home with the boys so that she could help them accept their loss. They did and, in time, with affection from everyone they were able to deal with their loss.

Glen was an outstanding athlete mainly in basketball. His basketball coach took him to Concord College where he was able to get an athletic scholarship to complete his college education.

I taught his two brothers also; all were upright citizens and Christians. One brother became a minister and teacher, and the other one was a principal of a junior high school in Virginia. Both brothers are now deceased.

Glen is a very talented individual. I would like very much to see his work in publication. I am now eighty-nine years old and trust that his works will be acceptable in public markets.

Thanks,

Ruby Meade Robinson

TUNES FROM THE TUG

Tunes from the Tug are carried by
the thin membrane covering its water,
Lyrics that can only be heard by
it's native sons and daughters.
While looking down at the river
when circumstances are just right,
Waves reach a crescendo and tunes
are released to the wind in flight.

Most of my tunes of the Tug
are deciphered from unscrambled words,
That was carried by currents of wind
and the songs of the birds.
I jotted partial tunes down when
tools for writing were near,
I missed some phrases and words
so I added memories of yesteryear.

Seems like no one listens for the
tunes from the Tug anymore,
'Cause it takes time and patience—
two virtues that exist no more.
Boyhood days we spent on the Tug
are hidden far back in our minds,
If those memories are not written,
forever, they'll be lost to mankind.

THE COAL MINER

Before the dawn he began putting
on his warm work clothes,
Today he was running late and it was
only minutes before the sun rose.
He picked up his old lunch bucket that

was lying on the kitchen floor,
Not to waken anyone his movements
were silent as he went out the door.

He could see the Seven Sisters slowly
fading in the northern sky,
And he felt the rumbling of a coal train
as it noisily passed by.
Towards the latter part of his mile walk
he increased the speed of his pace,
So he could catch up with the miners
walking toward the face.

He ran fast to the end of this long line
and arrived just in time,
The miners began to smell an odd odor
as they got deeper in the mine.
One of the miners lit their carbide light
and a terrible explosion occurred,
When finally the dust and smoke cleared
not a sound was heard.

All the miners on that shift were killed
in the explosion of the methane,
The accident could've easily been avoided
if workers were treated more humane.
It was the responsibility of the company
to keep the mine gas free,
Trying to save money the owner dismissed
the man in charge of safety.

There wasn't much a poor miner could do,
'cause grumbling would get him fired.
Often coal miners were put on a blacklist
and no where would they be hired.
The way the coal barons treated a miner
was second rate and sad,

They caused many injuries and deaths
and among them was my own Dad.

COAL CAMP

The river ran close to this treeless bottom
the land was always cold and damp,
The Coal Company had many workmen
that worked to build this coal camp.
In advance the Company ordered the
lumber from the sawmills around,
The Company built fifty solid
foundations upon this level ground.

The Company used seven handicapped
miners but only two carpenters were found,
Soon the shacks were built, though ugly
and imperfect, they were strong and sound.
Some whitewash made them look better
but it wouldn't keep the cold wind out,
Nor the heat of those summer days
when the flies and mosquitoes came about.

Now we had a shack at the coal camp
with a roof that didn't leak over our head,
All furniture were homemade items
such as tables, chairs and bunk-beds.
There was a big pot-bellied coal stove
that we burned to escape the cold,
From feed sacks Mom sewed curtains
to improve the looks of our household.

We were owned lock, stock and barrel
by the Company Store,
Debt for rent and necessities at that store
would always exist forevermore.

For the owner to control a miner
he made an indentured-servant type plan,
Which would take several years of work
for any miner to become a debt-free man.

The plan worked for a long while until
John L. Lewis and the Union came to stay,
And almost immediately the coal miners
were treated in a very different way.
An increase in pay was slow to come
and all hardships ended, but not overnight,
But the best of all that happened was
the coal miner got all of his inalienable rights.

Thanks to the Union for the brick home
that we live in today,
And all of those wonderful things
that somehow always came our way.
On one of the shelves out in the garage
sits my old tarnished carbide lamp,
Reminding me of mining and living
at that God-forsaken coal camp.

CARBIDE LAMP

Long before sunrise the miners
gathered at the entrance to embark,
For their long walk into the mine
when their path became pitch dark;
The coal-dust air and water seeping in
made breathing humid and damp,
They paused for just a few minutes
and lit their carbide lamp.

It was such a simple little lamp
that they carried every day,

4

It attached to their hard hat
in such a clever and unusual way.
When the carbide gas was lit by
a round grooved metal striking flint,
The spark ignited the gas into a light
that was quite fluorescent.

The coal miner worked on a quota
of loading so much coal per day,
If a miner didn't reach this goal
the Company would pro-rate his pay.
Miners helped each other load their quota
before going home to the coal camp,
But they could have never met any goal
without their carbide lamp.

THE ICEMAN

Roscoe had a big red
tarp-covered truck,
That hauled blocks of ice—
each block cost half-a-buck.
He got it from the ice plant in
Huntington on Route 52,
On those hot summer days
we're glad when he came thru.

Roscoe used the ice pick
with a surgeon's skill,
The chips of ice would fly
and into the truck they'd spill.
Large and small chips would start
to melt as they would fall,
We'd pick them up before
meltdown and eat them all.

Ice cost a penny a pound
which was a very good deal,
Families could not afford it
but a cool drink had a lot of appeal.
With his sharp steel tongs
he carried the ice to the icebox,
The ice weight and sharp ended
tongs made a carrying lock.

It became a nice cool time in our
little uncomplicated town,
When once a week we'd run
that big red ice truck down.
Ice water soothed our bare feet
as we ran over hot paved ground,
It was a happy and innocent age
and the best time ever found.

CIRCUS BALL

In the window was a
colorful circus ball,
The tag on it showed
10 cents (tax and all).
It was at Murphy's
a well known 10 cent store,
Painted on the ball were
wild animals galore.

There was a black seal
balancing a ball on its nose,
An enormous grey elephant
adorned with a saddle of rose.
A long-necked giraffe
yellow with spots of tan,
And a brownish lion

with mane of hair so grand.

Joe had a barn that leaned far
left and was about to fall,
It was strong with some oak
boards on the shady side wall.
Dad nailed the Karo syrup bucket
up because he was very tall,
Soon we were shooting buckets
with our circus ball.

We did a lot of shooting and
played a game we called "horse,"
and the champ was never
actually determined of course.
Winning was always plastered
in the front of our mind,
After losing we couldn't stand
the kidding and rubbing in time.

The Uptowners Uppities were
playing my Downtowner Dreams,
We were a whole lot better than
the much bigger Uppity team.
The game determined who had
bragging rights all over town.
It was only natural that we wanted
to beat the Uppities down.

The Uppities were leading 24 to 23
with seconds left in the game,
Anyone could be a hero that day
and never again feel the same.
"Shoot the ball!" "Shoot the ball!"
the fans began to yell.
Windy drove towards the bucket
tripped over a foot and fell.

The circus ball went into the air
and hit hard by the clover,
Bounced towards the bucket rim
went thru and the game was over.
We are still called poor sports
for the way we behaved that day,
We'd just smile and say "losers"
and go on our merry way.

Last summer while at the beach a
colorful ball came out of the sky,
It brought back vivid memories
of a wonderful time gone by.
I recalled the first day we shot
our colorful circus ball,
It was such a simple pleasure
that was enjoyed by us all.

SCHOOL'S OUT

All the young girls
were very sad,
And all the young boys
were joyful and glad;
Most of the girls cried
and some began to pout,
While the boys jumped with joy
and began to laugh and shout.

School's out! School's out!
Teacher wore her paddle out!
Summer had finally come
and soon there would be no doubt,
A time of freedom with
no bitter pills to swallow,
Just doing things our way

with few instructions to follow.

But, no matter how we approached
summer vacation wouldn't last,
The days of June, July, and August
progressed by so fast.
Our freedom days were numbered
and gone was the fun in the sun,
When the bell rang that fall
we knew it was time to learn.

A ditty we made up
as we made our way to school,
"We must learn to read again
momma didn't raise no fool.
And we must always try to follow
all the gosh-durn rules,
Because teacher's old oak paddle
is a good warning tool."

Today our ditty goes like this:
School's begun! School's begun!
Time to learn! Time to learn!
Our lives have made a terrible turn
for those carefree days we'll yearn.
But, school's begun! School's begun!
Time to learn! Time to learn!
Shoot…It's time to learn!

KNOCK THE CAN

We pranced on summer nights
foot loose and fancy free,
Playing under the street light
so we might be able to see.
We called our pal Joey

the broomstick man,
'Cause he was hard to beat
in our game of knock-the-can.

Joey was slender with long strides
and faster than a deer he ran,
Quickly from the dark he'd appear
with his broomstick in hand.
And with one mighty swing
he'd knock all the cans,
Then faster than he appeared
he escaped into the darkened land.

The rules of the knock-the-can
had always been the same,
But no one really knows
for we never finished a game.
No one cared if they lost
it was just some pastime play,
With some wonderful friends
in those youthful days.

BUD THE KING OF MARBLES

Bud bought some marbles
from the town's new grocery,
Then broke a branch off
a flowering crabapple tree.
He borrowed from Dan
some strong twine string,
The string and branch were used
to draw a marble ring.

With just a few exceptions
the ring was perfectly round,
Bud put 25 of his marbles

in the middle of the even ground.
He said, "Anti-up 25 marbles with
mine—if you want to play,
The marbles can be good or bad
'cause I will pocket them today."

In an hour we had lost our
"cat-eyes," "smoothies," and all.
Bud could shoot arrow straight
or curve it like a baseball.
He could make the marble spin
or reverse it into a draw.
A book should be written about
the skill of Bud and his "Taw."

In the Heavenly Sports Pavilion
sits the King Of All Things,
Close by is Jack Dempsey, king of
boxing and champion in the ring.
Also Dick Buttons, the ice king—
and king Elvis ready to sing;
And playing marbles is Bud—
king of the marble ring.

CORNSILK SMOKING

I found the old brown poke
it was torn and tattered.
Jim got the matches from the
stove which was splattered—
With the hot gravy that Mom
made early before sunrise.
From the plate on that stove
we got us some fried pies.

We sneaked out of the house

and ran towards the old barn.
We knew we'd get the switch—
but didn't really give a darn.
We hurried to the cornfield
where ears were silk ripe.
Jim put black cornsilk into
gramps old cobblestone pipe.

Lit up, relaxed, and puffing,
he soon blew a smoke ring.
I got the poke, the cornsilk,
didn't need one more thing.
Quickly I rolled a cigarette
twixt my fingers and my thumb,
Twisted the ends hard
and swiped it with my tongue.

On the ground I made a bed
of hay which was new-mown.
Smoked and slept until noon—
when all the makin's were gone.
We ran fast to the corn patch
as gray smoke blew out the door.
We enjoyed the cornsilk so much
we had to have some more.

Gramps was in the porch swing
as he often was before.
He whacked us both with his cane
it hurt him to the core.
Funny, but I still can't figure out—
Which did it hurt more?
He looked at us in a stern way,
and said, "Don't do it anymore!"

We are both old men now
on the last visit I had with Jim.

We had the desire to try
cornsilk smoking again.
Jim got the brown bag
the other stuff was up to me.
Just a few puffs made us agree
it wasn't as good as it used to be.

MUMBLETY-PEG

If the temperature reached 90
as it was in August about every day,
We met at the railroad depot porch
because it was shady and we'd play.
You must have a balanced knife that
you'd borrowed with a pleasing beg,
It had to be a strong and sturdy knife
to play the game of mumblety-peg.

Two blades of the knife were opened
and the sharp ends were exposed,
One blade was opened all the way
and one blade was half closed.
Balancing the back of the knife on the
forefinger and resting it on a thumb,
The knife was flipped into the air and
if it stuck up you didn't feel so dumb.

The knife sticking up on the long blade
was worth twenty-five points to you,
If the two blades both stuck—
to fifty points the total grew.
If for some reason the knife should
land on its back and not turn over,
The flipper of the knife had won
and the game was now over.

The game went to five hundred
and playing it was a great pastime,
It was a game that was free
and you didn't spend one dime.
Those were unique days
and I made friends of a special kind,
They are really true friends and I see
them from time to time.

After losing at mumblety-peg all day
I walked down the railroad track,
And a tiny ray of light from behind
many rocks came shining back.
As I pilfered among the rocks
the best thing happened to me,
I saw the beautiful sight of a
new Barlow pretty as could be.

Finding that knife was good luck
for I went on a winning spree,
I hardly ever lost at mumblety-peg
becoming champ of the county.
As I became older other interests
seemed much closer to my heart,
No longer did the game appeal
to me and we soon drifted apart.

There is still the base for the rails
but the railroad depot is gone,
It's now just a big parking lot
paved with rocks and stone.
Mumblety-peg was lost to progress
a game that was outgrown,
Mumblety-peg is for the ages,
and for most people unknown.

FUDGE

On the top of houses in town
smoke rose out of the chimney,
The coal fire burned hot
atop the wood from a pine tree.
The pungent smell of sulfur
permeated the snow laden air,
Gas mantels were lit
and windows showed a red glare.

We gathered at the kitchen table
we were all playing 500 rummy,
Bill tongued and licked his lips
and rubbed around on his tummy.
Alma with her right elbow quickly
gave young Bill a forceful nudge,
He sheepishly asked the question,
"Mom, how 'bout making some fudge?"

Mom did not heed the question
she went straight to the kitchen,
She carried the leftovers to our table
some gravy and fried chicken.
Put some sugar, cocoa, and cream
into her old aluminum pot,
Stoked the wood burning stove
until the lids were red hot.

Mom didn't measure one item
all ingredients she just poured in,
We smelled the aromatic mixture
it made us twitch our nose and grin.
Often stirring the candy, then suddenly,
it was finished up real soon,
Bill and me got to lick the pan
Alma and Linda were given the spoon.

In just a few minutes Mom brought
the fudge in two large plates,
It was all gone in a jiffy
for the taste was so great.
If only a company like Hershey
would have gotten her recipe,
But it's in Heaven's file cabinet
that only Mom can see.

HORSESHOES

One dusky evening as I walked
the railroad tracks to town,
I could hear a clanking noise
like a metal against metal sound.
I kept hearing the clanking
until I reached an abandoned lot,
When I saw the horseshoe pegs
I knew I was at the clanging spot.

The town council spent some of
their dollars to give us some light.
Charlie climbed high on the pole
and positioned them just right.
They cast an eerie shadow
and they were somewhat bright,
The horseshoe pit was so nice
pitching in the cool of the night.

When the curfew siren sounded
and ended its shrieking shout,
Our game ended immediately
and all lights were turned out.
The horseshoe games were over
and it was a wonderful day,
After breakfast we'd try it again
and hope victory was our play.

The sun rose early the next day
and a heavy dew was in the air,
All four of the horseshoes
were still there, plus the spare.
And the sound we began hearing
was that metal clanking again,
As that wonderful challenge
of the horseshoe pit began.

If you're driving in the country
and you hear that clanking sound,
Or walking through the city park
and there are horseshoe pits around.
No matter which way you've traveled
one could venture a guess and say,
"That those who pitched horseshoes
were relaxed and had a happy day."

DANDELIONS

Hundreds of dandelions growing
all over the hill,
Yellow golden buttons
shining in green velvet fields.

Quickly the breath of angels blows
a round gray seed-pod,
Into the air as if guided
by the hand of God.

Soon new golden buttons growing
change to gray bublettes showing,
Along breezy paths they're flying
God's plan for renewing.

A puff of air made by you
will make the seeds fly into,

17

A waiting sky of blue
and make dreams come true.

TWILIGHT IN THE VALLEY

The sun is about to peak
over an Appalachian hill,
The darkness is disappearing
from its hush of silent still.
The sky is slowing turning
into a red-bluish hue,
The greenery of the mountain
is beginning to show thru.

Suddenly, along the valley
up to the top of the hill,
A rooster call reverberates
across a twilight rill.
Sounding a wake-up call
of a "Cock-a-doodle-do!"
Which in rooster talk means
"Good morning to you!"

NUDIST COLONY

A nudist colony formed on Marrowbone Creek,
so, around the mountain I thought I'd sneak.
Snow was in the air and the sky looked bleak,
but I knew that it'd be worthwhile if I'd get a peak.

As I approached the spot that I'd tried to seek.
My eyes stared in amazement and I could not speak.
Hurriedly I ran closer, like an Olympic sprinter,
only to see a sign that read, "Clothed for the winter."

MY WISH

If I had but—
one more wish,
I'd like to go to my place
on the Tug to fish.
With some homebrew
in an old milk jug,
And a nice built lady
that I could hug.

Nowhere on Earth
would I rather be-
Than under the shade of
that old sycamore tree.
'Tis my special place
so peaceful and still,
I'll miss it one day—
I know I will.

MEMORIES

Many places we remember
from those years long ago,
Many faces we still see
that we used to know.
Many rare occurrences—
in our mind still last,
Reminders of our roots
from a childhood past.

Memories printed indelibly
upon our minds marquee,
Common recollections
of those days carefree.
We shared a path together

down an old memory avenue,
And never, ever forgot-
the true friends that we knew.

We remember the call
of a lonely whippoorwill,
And the sound of a bobwhite—
echoing from a hill.
We remember the locomotives
on the N&W tracks,
Belching out cinders and smoke
from their long black stacks.

We recall times at the depot
where games were played,
Of Oscar's and The Fountain
where we often stayed.
We think of the cool water
from the pump of Pa Baker.
And those scary telegrams
delivered by Mr. Staker.

We remember the Tug River
that gave us so much pleasure,
As we swam and fished
'twas a poor boy's treasure.
We reminisce of the Big Bottom
where we'd laugh and shout.
Then run to the Sand Bar,
where we'd lay out.

We have memories of the Tipple.
Dan's and the old Cash Store,
The Lock-Up, Post Office,
and many, many more.
But our fondest memory
of those days gone by,

Were of all our good friends
at dear old Kermit High.

STUMP

The water pumped from the river
was 5,000+ gallons of water/hour,
It was stored in a high place
called the cooling tower.
The tower's water, cooled
all pumps which got very hot,
Then the hot water went
to the river in a very nice spot.

The hot water flowed gently
and into the cold water it'd bump,
There the water turned tepid
as it ran by our diving stump.
Big Bill was a tall feller
and was pleasingly plump,
He quit the belly bust dive
and did the cannonball jump.

Now, Red was the best diver
that ever dove at the stump,
He'd arch his back perfectly
and show only his white rump.
He'd enter the water smoothly
without a splash nor thump,
And if the dive was not perfect
he became an old grump.

There is no accurate description
of how we had so much diving fun,
And playing all the water games
in that wonderful Tug River sun.

I'll never forget those times and
I know that I am not the only one,
For whenever old friends meet
a stump diving discussion is begun.

The older boys held us under
and splashed water in our eyes,
We had some great memories and
later loved most of those guys.
There were no sandbar loafers
for they would throw you in,
And they continued this practice
until we all learned to swim.

The leader would often say to us,
"You're going to drown or swim!"
When the leader of the group
said such things—we listened to him.
But, we have to admit before long
we learned to swim, dive and jump,
For we were taught the hard way
at our favorite spot the stump.

Nowadays, there are diving boards
at all of the swimming pools,
There are Red Cross trained lifeguards
and nameless safety tools.
There's whistles constantly blowing
for the slightest rule infractions,
Gone forever is "skinny dipping"
and all that stump diving action.

HOMEMADE ICE CREAM

Long ago and far away
I thought of a time of yesterday,

During some very hot weather
that was unusual for May.
I looked over the fence
from the side of my house,
Ora Ellen was making ice cream
at the home of Mrs. Rouse.

I jumped the fence quickly
it was only about 4 feet high.
I looked at everyone that
seemed to be standing by.
Bob Rouse made the best
homemade ice cream in town,
I grabbed the wooden handle
ready to turn it around.

Alva had made the fixings then—
stirred it 'til 'twas like velvet,
She gently poured the mixture
into the metal bucket.
The container lid and
turning paddle all locked in place,
The cranking was about to begin
and a smile came to Bob's face.

Rock salt and ice were put in
and for awhile it sloshed around,
Soon a frosty white smoke arose
and drifted to the ground.
Then the ice cream was checked
and some canned peaches put in.
In a minute it was ready
and soon the eating was to begin.

I turned the crank of the ice cream
maker all the time that day,
Some old memories are vanishing

and some are about to fade away.
Often I think of the many treats
that I greatly enjoyed as a lad,
But the homemade ice cream made
that day was the best I ever had.

A 1,000 POINTS OF LIGHT

On a spring night
before the dew sat in,
Tiny specks of light no bigger
than the end of a pin.
Would flicker on and off
over and over again,
'Twas the lightning bugs
that had a light built in.

In a pitch black night
when the humidity is high,
Lots of erratic spots of light
are low in the sky.
But for some reason
and no one knows why?
Less of them can be seen
when the night is dry.

Not like embers of a fire
that go high and lose their glow,
Lightning bugs have no order
and flickers everywhere they go.
Small amounts of light is given
when they just fly around,
The brighter their light becomes
the closer it is to the ground.

Once we collected lightning bugs

and put them in a jar,
Released them all at once
they were like a shooting star.
Reminded me of President Bush's speech
about, "A thousand points of light."
And we saw most of those points
on that magnificent night.

RIDING THE SAGE

We'd walk thru the sagebrush
to "shoo" away pheasants,
Under an autumn blue sky
with air so pleasant.
It was a time in life
which was our danger age,
We'd dodge everything
when we rode the sage.

We'd bend the sage over
until it laid down,
And with some cardboard
we'd ride the ground.
Sagebrush was a low shrub
that grew on a dry hill,
When you rode the slick sage
it'd give you a thrill.

A long piece of cardboard
that would seat about eight,
All of our gang would think
the ride was fast and great.
We got our cardboard
from the 'frigerator store,
We also rode on linoleum
from a vacant house floor.

We'd hang on to one another
as we came down the hill,
Sometimes it would keep us
from having a hurtful spill.
We had a contest against
anybody in our town,
We'd race them all—
and no team put us down.

Riding the sage hurt when
it tossed you to and fro,
Today it'd probably kill us
for that was a time long ago.
I would try to ride the sage
even at this time and day,
But my bones are too brittle
and my courage has turned gray.

WADING IN THE CREEK

Spring was about over
and summer wasn't for a week,
But I took my shoes off
and waded in the creek.
I was in the 4th grade
and about 10 years old,
The creek was not deep
but it sure was cold.

That day I splashed and
thru the water I'd run,
Laughing all the way
a time of great fun.
Got the weight off my
shoulders that seemed a ton,
It was so relaxing and nice

as my feet dried in the sun.

One day I saw a sandpiper
with long legs so sleek,
And with a quick movement
of its long, sharp beak—
Pulled out a minnow
and flew off like a streak.
It was a lovely moment
for me as I waded the creek.

I saw many salamanders
and crawdads pinched my toes,
The mud relaxed my feet
in a way nobody knows.
Water bugs floated over
the water spring-fed clear,
And a lot of dragon flies
buzzed me so very near.

When troubles are greatest
and it's only Monday of your week,
Search your mind for neurons
for memories of peace to seek.
Locked in part of your cerebrum
at a time when life seems bleak.
Your troubles might be erased if—
once more you'd wade a creek.

MY FIRST CHEW

Down by the riverside
Uncle Bud's tobacco grew,
Where the sun blazed all day
and a cool river breeze blew.
It was the finest stand

of tobacco you ever did see,
And the best thing of all,
a person could chew free.

If one used tobacco habitually
they were a "tobacco hound."
All my childhood friends
with whom I ran around—
Chewed tobacco constantly
whether uptown or down.
One day while running our
way thru the tobacco ground.

Jim said, "Take a chew of tobacco
or I will knock you down."
Jim was bad, but I think I was
ready to try it anyhow.
He picked a handful of selected
leaves from all around,
I put them in my jaw and it left a
taste the worst I'd ever found.

Jim said, "Don't spit it out!
You got to try it awhile."
He said it through stained
teeth and an infrequent smile.
I was doing a little better
as my tobacco began to wet,
I knew that I did not like it—
and I never would, I bet.

This experience with tobacco
for me was brand new,
Learning the unexpected
when I had my first chew.
My best friend slipped up
behind and gave me a whack,

I swallowed my tobacco
from that blow to my back.

My head began to feel woozy
and over my stomach turned.
My abdomen was upset
and the gastric juices churned.
There's irritation in my mouth
and my taste buds burned.
I heaved up for a long time
it was a lesson well learned.

As the years passed by
my yearning for tobacco grew,
It had become a habit for me
and more and more I'd chew.
One day I quit "cold turkey"
it was really tough for me.
Never get that nasty habit
or you might never get free.

SUNDAY SCHOOL

When I was a young boy
it was a job for Granny to see,
That I knew that Sunday School
was something expected of me.
Pretending to be sick and crocodile
tears would simply not work.
I knew early that my obligation
to Sunday School I couldn't shirk.

When the church bell rang
I had only minutes to get ready,
Up to now putting on my Sunday
best had been slow but steady.

I got there a few minutes late
and only heard the word Pharisee.
Then, we all began to sing—
the old tune, "Jesus Loves Me!"

Some of the stories I heard
in Sunday School I'll never forget,
It's like they were told yesterday
and I remember them vividly yet.
Stories about people in the Bible
the one about Moses shook my soul—
And why I remember that one
so clearly only God knows.

Sunday School help mold me
into what I have become today.
Though as a youngster I drifted
down the path of moral decay.
I now keep the commandments
for I know it is the only way.
And I pray I've done enough
on my Judgment Day.

Think what's best for children
"don't be stubborn as a mule."
Children need love, character,
and morals just as much as you.
Let them at least hear and
practice the Golden Rule.
They'll have a better life if
they go to Sunday School.

PUMPING STATION

Vomp pwa shoop—Vomp pwa shoop
was the duplicating and irritating sound,

That constantly echoed
thru the streets and alleys of our town.
Minute by minute
it soon became a mental disruption.
Our little pumping station
that sent natural gas all over the nation.

Vomp pwa shoop—Vomp pwa shoop
Like the noise of a band troupe.
Sounds out of a space movie
that drowned out jukebox music so groovy.
Hour by hour
a metal mechanical heart beat a rhythmic tune.
Day and night
echoing in the hills under an Appalachian moon.

Vomp pwa shoop—Vomp pwa shoop
a thunderous sound that made sleepy eyes droop.
Week after week
interrupting neighbors talking on their stoop.
Year after year
covering their ears as they met as a group.
Decade after decade
hearing the monotonous sound of Vomp pwa shoop.

Years later I came back home and showed
off my Chevy coupe—
Noticing now that silence prevailed up town
and around the loop.
Saddened by silence, then happily I gave out a
Tug Valley whoop.
Much louder than the pumping station sound of
Vomp pwa shoop—Vomp pwa shoop.

BLACKBERRY PICKING

It was twilight in the mountains
so peaceful and so still,
And a beautiful red sunrise
was coming over Man's Face hill.
Occasionally a songbird
would sing in a voice so shrill,
Figuring out what bird it was
would give you an inner thrill.

I was comfortably sitting
on nature's mattress on my tush,
I got up on my knees beside
a large blackberry bush.
There was plenty of light now
and it was easy to see,
Momma didn't raise no fool
when she raised me.

Often coiled copperheads
that you could not see,
Lay under those berry bushes
ready to strike a hand or knee.
But through the day long
there was nary a one,
The berry pickin' was tiresome
but I was thru before the hot sun.

I picked 'til my bucket was full
my fingers sore from briars a stickin',
I remember that day in the berry patch for
'twas next to the last day I went berry pickin'.
I knew that when Granny got 'em
flavor miracles happened when she'd bake,
A pan of golden brown berry cobbler
and her tasty jellyroll cake.

Nothing like those blackberries
can you buy anymore,
Those were bigger with more flavor
than those you buy in the store.
The last time I went berry pickin'
I took my girlfriend Mary Lou,
Later we married by that berry patch
and became one instead of two.

GRAPEVINE

In the rolling mountains
where the possum grapes grow,
Small tasty bunches hang
in pods high on the vine in a row.
You can climb high
pick 'em and drop 'em to the ground.
Or you can throw rocks
until you knock some down.

The grapevine grows
from the ground to the top of the tree.
The vine entwines itself
and becomes strong as can be.
You can immediately see
a new world if you dare to swing,
From the long grapevine delve
into a blue sky where flying birds sing.

Should you have the nerve
look left and right at the far below,
Things that used to be so tall,
Appearing in this vortex glow
now seems very small.
Ascend high into a sky of blue,
up and up, on a nature made swing—

that'll take the breath out of you.

Ride that grapevine once more
used stored imagination if you have too.
Let memories return of youthful days
those that were favorites to you.
Remembering when there were no worries
and free was your soul, body and mind.
Please, ride that grapevine again
for it may be your last time.

HERE COMES JOHN DUNN

If Stark Brothers would have
known a way back then—
That a tree like this would
fetch a lot of money in.
I'm sure they would have
had a patent on this tree,
For 'twas the best June apple
that there could ever be.

How that tree got there is
something only God would know,
It must have mutated and
by the river it began to grow.
We'd go thru Flossie's land
for sneaking was so much fun.
We'd jump a short picket fence
to the yard of John Dunn.

John wouldn't let us pick up
the apples lying on the ground.
Nor did he like the idea of us
using rocks to knock 'em down.
But by the time of our raid

John Dunn was not around,
He was in the mailroom
at the Post Office up town.

John left for work before nine
so our invasion began about ten.
Only seconds later we had
apple juice running down our chin.
The apple was light green with
a slight tint of red on the peel.
They made cobblers and pies
the taste was almost unreal.

That day we ate so many apples
most of us began to feel ill,
But suddenly we had to skedaddle
and show only a fast moving heel.
That June apple day spent with a
lot of friends was great fun.
It ended when we heard, "Run!
Run! Run! Here comes John Dunn."

There in all her majesty that
apple tree grew for years alone,
But now for many unknown
reasons it to time is gone.
There is not even a stump
of our delicious June apple tree,
That wonderful mutated creation
is lost forever to eternity.

THE DREADED STUFF

Sometimes I thought it punishment
and sometimes I thought it not.
And sometimes a big spoonful

of that dreaded stuff I got.
It made my face grimace and
to my inners it was rough.
I just could not get my stomach
to enjoy that dreaded tasting stuff.

The smell was pungent to the nose
the fumes would make you cry.
The taste of that colorless liquid
made you think you'd surely die.
Whether feeling constipated and "puny"
or symptoms of the deadly "flu,"
Granny would force the dreaded stuff
down—a tablespoon or two.

Yesterday I went to three
different drug stores,
Found out that none of them
carried it anymore.
I knew of one old store
way out in the country.
The druggist said, "There just
might be some in aisle C."

I finally found it by the black
salve used to treat a boil,
There were only two dusty
bottles of the castor oil.
I knew that this awful stuff
ought to be free,
I bought both of the bottles—
tax and all it came to $7.93.

I opened the lid and the odor
and taste was as it used to be.
Memories came back instantly
and I sat on Granny's knee.

She held my nose and arms
so I could not get free,
Mom gave a heaping tablespoon
of the dreaded stuff to me.

They're no words to describe
about the dreaded stuff.
I have to admit that it helped
when my sickness got so rough.
It made my stomach ache
and my heart began to toil,
After just taking a spoonful
of that awful castor oil.

MOUNTAIN SPRING

Through the woods I went
with the bucket in my hand.
Traipsing thru the mayapple
where the paw paws stand.
In the damp shady land
where the ginseng grows,
A new spring began to flow
just a few short days ago.

Who found this eternal spring?
We don't think we'll ever know.
News of the spring didn't take
long for the word to grow.
Our old and closest spring
was about to reach its demise.
Our jug was slow to fill
With water that you'd despise.

The new spring flowed fast
and its water was crystal clear.

In minutes you'd fill a bucket
with no taste and smell so pure.
It's the only good water there was—
we pray there is never a drought.
And this river of ground water
will never change its route.

But in one day our needed
and loved spring disappeared.
Our water supply dried up—
'tis something we had feared.
No longer could be heard
its flow thru the grassy ground.
The water plant became the answer
it pumped water to all in town.

Today there is Pepsi, 7-Up,
Coca Cola, and Mountain Dew.
And water that is imported
clear as a crystal too.
But all the drinks ever made
can't compare to the king-
For it was perfect waters that
Came from our mountain spring.

POTION

If you are older than dirt
like some of us have gotten to be,
While walking thru the woods
And you see a bluebird or chickadee.
Then your chances are very high
you've just passed a sassafras tree,
Look closely for it grows in clumps
and may be camouflaged by shrubbery.

Remove most of the sassafras roots
with careful nursery surgery,
Let Ma boil the roots a long time
using her acquired caldron sorcery.
When the potion turns dark brown
it makes a wonderful tasting recipe,
And it tastes even better when flavored
with mint, rock-candy, and whiskey.

After taking two teaspoons of this potion,
those that have, always seem to agree,
That they have a feeling of Capt. Marvel
where once they were sick as could be.
Arguments have often risen about the
medicinal value of sassafras tea,
I don't care what others might say
but the potion surely helped me.

MY MOUNTAIN IS GONE

We were on the mountain hunting
our dog "Speed," Dad and me,
"Speed" sniffed the brown grasses
and sagebrush much taller than he.
Out jumped two "cottontails" and
down different paths began to flee
Bam! Bam! Went Dad's 12 gauge
he was accurate as could be.

My emotions were all shattered
and I was visibly shaken,
When Dad picked up the two rabbits
whose lives were just taken.
My heart skipped a beat and
gnawing in my stomach grew,
But then everything got okay

39

when Ma made the rabbit stew.

The last time I traveled down
to my mountain home,
I saw rabbits scurrying around
but my mountain was gone.
My dog "Speed" was over 18
and had eaten his last bone,
He is buried with Ma and Pa
on some flat-ground overgrown.

I know that soon there will
be a reckoning time a coming,
When all mountains are gone
and no sound of wind humming.
And the moon will always rise
over a non-existent hill,
I will miss those old memories
I just know that I will.

DOC JONES

I have an imaginary friend
that I call Doc Jones,
He talks now and then with me
and then he is gone.
Sometimes he taps my shoulder
when I'm deep in thought alone,
It's when I'm busy writing
and he tells me what is wrong.

It's usually in the darkest night
while everyone else is asleep,
He whispers to me about
a word to delete or keep.
I have no idea when Doc Jones

will suddenly in my mind leap.

Years ago my mind was very
free to think and to roam,
But now it's locked within myself
into Alzheimer I have gone.
My outer being has crumbled and
my face became a pallor stone,
I mentally talk with God
for He really is Doc Jones.

HOBO STEW

The freight train chugged slowly
into the railroad yard,
Night was a coming on fast
and times were really hard.
The boxcar was barely moving
as he made the climb down,
His legs were half asleep
as he trotted upon the ground.

The night was now a deep dark
and the air was cool and damp,
He walked towards the river
where there was a hobo camp.
He was in total black dark
'til he saw the candlelight.
Seeing him, I asked, "Is there
room for one more hobo tonight?"

He replied, "Welcome stranger
pull up a piece of damp ground,
Empty yourself of your load
and lay or sit yourself down."
In a black kettle on the fire an

41

aroma arose smelled only by a few,
He gave me a generous portion
of his wonderful hobo stew.

Lots of hoboes were professional men
that had run out of all their luck,
They rode the rails to escape boredom
for there were no jobs to earn a buck.
Someday he knew that he would return
no matter whatever he had to do,
To where the old hobo "hangs"
and eat some more of his hobo stew.

COLOR RHAPSODY

There is a beautiful song in nature
that does not have a note or tune,
It's all around us if we should look-
'twas made by God before the moon.

Black flying wings with orange dots
'tis the colorful monarch butterfly,
It carefully lands on a yellow dandelion
in the light-green lawn close by.

A non-resting dark-blue hummingbird
beaking into a purple morning glory,
And a flight of yellow-black honeybees
working green clover on a nectar spree.

The reddest cardinal atop an indigo mum
searching for a light-tan seed or two,
And a long slender light-green garter snake
tonguing the pink rose it slithers through.

Don't forget those varying red sunsets

and those white puffy clouds above,
All are but a part of God's color rhapsody
that's unwritten with no notes we all love.

CLAYTOR LAKE

There is a valley of the New River
where a dam was built from side to side,
Not for hydroelectric power
but for the recreation it could provide.
Virginia thought about the future
and wisely set the land aside,
A spot nature and Heaven exists harmoniously—
and from life for awhile you can hide.

The wind from the lake was invisible
as it pathed thru the trees,
How much the leaves rustled
varied with the strength of the breeze.
There were a few rhythmic ripples
that constantly lapped the lake-shore,
And the same ripples seemed to intensify
as the wind blew harder and constantly more.

In moments several colorful sailboats
came out of a protected hidden cove,
Guided by the powerful wind from the east
to the west an unseen navigator drove.
Scaring the beautiful colored mallard ducks
into "V" formation winging thru a blue sky,
A magnificent sight to many lakeside swimmers
and hikers that watched from a crest nearby.

If you happen to be a water sports enthusiast
there are so many things to do,
Like using a jet-ski, sailing, kayaking, boating,

canoeing or learning to water-ski too.
For swimmers there is a diving platform
only feet from sunbathers on a sandy beach,
For fishermen there's a special cove
that takes only a few minutes to reach.

There's nature all around you everywhere
as you hike along the many trails,
You'll see squirrels, rabbits, deer and
most birds even pheasant and quail.
Should you want a relaxed and peaceful time
visit the State Park at Claytor Lake,
It will be a time well spent
and unforgettable memories you'll make.

GINSENG

Uncle Joey was in the mountains
with a knapsack on his back,
A mattock and a shovel
was hanging from his pack.
The shade hit the may-apple
and all the things around,
It was in such a meadow
where ginseng could be found.

Under the leaves were many plants
of 'seng that could weigh pounds,
Using his shovel he dug deep and
pulled the roots from the ground.
Astonished the roots were so large
the area had not been dug before,
They'd bring a lot of money when sold
to the druggist down at his store.

The term "Ginsengologist" has been

coined for hunters of the "seng,"
'Twas a person scouring woods for fun
and the money the plants would bring.
"Old Timers" like Uncle Joey walked
through the mountains each day,
It was mostly recreation for him
in a healthy, enjoyable way.

MILKING TIME

I went over hill and dale
thru stickweeds and wildflowers,
I looked in nooks and crannies
for more than a frazzling hour.
My heart jumped with joy
when I saw hoof-prints around,
The cool, marshy, wetlands
where lilies and cattails abound.

Escaping the heat so harsh
she lay in the cooling mud,
Her big eyes moved back and forth
her mouth was chewing her cud.
Lazily and with quite a struggle
she got from the muddy ground,
Once white as flakes of snow—
she looked a muddy-brown.

Old Bossy's sack was milk-filled
and if events would possibly allow,
There was time enough yet
for Ma to milk this cow.
After filling over two buckets
Ma took time to wipe her brow,
Old Bossy gave the rich milk
and Ma supplied the know-how.

PERSIMMONS

The air was frosty
but the sun was so warm,
Hundreds of yellow jackets
flew about in a swarm.
I picked up the persimmons
didn't want any that's green,
Put 'em in my pocket for later—
all those colored in-between.

I ate some of the ripe ones
they were delicious to me,
Each one tasted better than
they were supposed to be.
One of the persimmons
looked ripe but was green,
My lips puckered up tighter
than any drum you've seen.

With my lips big and puckered
into a contorted display,
I headed for home to look
in the mirror right away.
There's no swelling of the lips
that could be seen,
The lesson learned was never
eat a persimmon that's green.

MOLASSES

If you happen to own
any rich creek-bank land,
Then it's easy to grow
a tall sugar cane stand.
Plow and furrow the soil

then plant the cane shoots,
Not deep in the fertile ground
and soon they will sprout roots.

When trees begin to lose leaves
and the cold air ushers in fall,
The cane which now shades
the sun is over 10-feet tall.
The cane should be cut
long before the winter snow,
Then fast to Ferguson's farm
by horse and wagon it must go.

There the cane is pulverized and
its creamed-colored juice runs down,
And it's caught in a metal container
just before it reaches the ground.
There are two large stones
that pulverize the sugar cane,
A horse pulls a long pole that
turns the large stones without strain.

The sugar cane juice is boiled until
it becomes molasses thick and brown,
Then carefully poured in jars
that are sold to stores in town.
A jar of molasses would last all
winter if you didn't use it everyday,
My Grandma knew how to use the
molasses in her own special way.

She would spoon out a dab or two
into her black wrought iron pan,
When the molasses got hot
she'd add a pinch of soda with her hand.
Miraculously turning the ingredients
into a bubbling creamy foam,

Sweet biscuit sopping syrup
better than honeycomb.

The kitchen aroma of fresh baked
molasses cookies we loved so well,
And the sizzling sound of those flapjacks
spread with molasses tasted so swell.
We didn't have much in those days
that seems so long ago and far.
We didn't have pennies to buy
a fancy wrapped Mars candy bar.

Any thing made of molasses
filled our sweet-tooth desire,
Granny would drizzle molasses
on corn popped over an open fire.
At Wal-Mart last week I looked
for molasses for sometime,
If molasses is about to disappear
it would be a terrible crime.

INDEPENDENCE DAY

Rarely did a circus
ever come to our town,
But, about twice a year
the carnival came around.
Front-men tacked posters
to anything of wood found,
Signs about the carnival
and riding the merry-go-round.

Everything was in its place
as we celebrated the 4th of July,
The day was so magnificent
and thrill of anticipation was high.

It was low temperature wise
under a few clouds and blue sky,
All things were now in motion
as we excitedly circled by.

A red, white and blue décor
adorned the make-shift stand,
And some volunteers patriotically
played songs that were so grand.
About America, freedom and love
we had for our glorious land,
We stopped to applaud vigorously
the Norma Hale's Pep Band.

We celebrated Independence Day
it was a time of family fun,
As the memorable hours passed by
night brought the fireworks on.
A lot of firecrackers exploding
and the rockets lit up the sky,
The time for the carnival was over
and we said a sorrowful goodbye.

During the early morning fog
the rides and booths were torn down,
All were loaded in the trucks
that soon left an empty ground.
Except for the cleaning crew
that was sprucing up all around,
There were tears shed as the carnival
trucks left our little town.

PAW PAWS

Through a cool shady nook
over a low moving brook,

A mountain breeze flows
'tis where the paw paws grow.

Led down a timeless trail
by the echoing of a distant bell,
To a green mattress canopy
and a clump of paw paw trees.

Paw paws were lying erratically
tasted delicious to me,
I spit the big seeds out
so they'd take root and sprout.

Now you can't find a paw paw
at any nursery or mall,
The mystic flavor that's unique
is about to become extinct.

But someday the paw paws
will begin to grow once more,
In clumps of trees very small
in a place they grew before.

WHITTLING

A group of old timers
about every single day,
Would gather at the lock-up
and whittle the hours away.
All that's required is a
knife that was very sharp,
And a block of dry wood
that was kept under a tarp.

Clancy cut only the best timber
from the trees on Meade hill,

He cut the whittling blocks
easy at his new sawmill.
Clancy cut different shapes
and sizes of hard and soft wood,
Graded them and stacked them
as superior, fine, and good.

There were two benches and
cane chairs that were homemade,
Each day the seats were filled
as the men whittled in the shade.
Each man chose his own wood
and soon the shavings would fly.
The shavings were light to medium
and the piles were inches high.

While whittling they'd gossip
and discuss the current news,
It was a round table discussion
and everyone offered his views.
They enjoyed the everyday
companionship with each other.
If weather stopped the whittling
they sorely missed one another.

The men whittled about everything
it could be any figure from A to Z,
Often carving some mental shapes
conceived in thought and memory.
The most magnificent whittler
was a man called Blind Bill,
He had the greatest imagination
and had to feel to gain his skill.

Many of the figures they whittled
are still down at the City Hall,

And some of those gentlemen's
pictures adorn the chamber wall.
Seemed those wonderful old timers
we didn't appreciate their worth;
Was the greatest group of whittlers
ever found on God's green earth.

WHATCHAMACALLIT

I was but a poor country boy
that became a celebrity,
People by the dozens came
to the fair just to see me.
From places far and wide
crowds came from all about,
They wanted to see me pull
my whatchamacallit out.

To show the whole world
a national treasure.
Some carpenters would
bring a tape measure,
That way they could prove
to those that might have doubt,
Of its girth and length, when I
pulled my whatchamacallit out.

Engineers and rail workers
would see me by the score,
Lots of fans wanted a repeat
of the time I pulled it out before.
Tile workers needed a tool
that would easier replace grout,
Some of them were around when I
pulled my whatchamacallit out.

This story began when I was
wounded four times in the war,
My mind would often leave me
and wasn't as good as before.
Instead of giving me 4 Purple Hearts
they gave me one big one to flount,
I always forgot the name Purple Heart
so, I pulled my whatchamacallit out.

RUBBER GUNS

The great depression was
nearing its horrific end,
There was not much to do
but lots of time to do it in.
We made up our own games
so we could have lots of fun,
The game we liked the best
was playing rubber guns.

Out behind Mike's old garage
he changed oil and gave lubes,
And if we were lucky enough
we'd find a rubber inner tube.
With a pair of granny's scissors
we'd cut 'til the bands were round,
They'd easily fit on our gun
and their stretch had no bounds.

I pretended to be on "Champion"
and was riding the cattle trail,
When I heard a sudden whack
and felt a sting upon my tail.
It was then I saw my friend Buddy
hiding behind the berry bush,
He was all full of smiles

when he shot me on the tush.

Rubber guns were easy to make
and such wonderful fun to play,
The rules changed frequently
but to most of us it was okay.
We played the game all the time
each and every day,
We'd meet in the big bottom
after church on a Sunday.

Dad lost his job at the mine
about the middle of May,
It was a lackluster time and I
couldn't think of much to say.
Their rubber gun aim was bad
for they missed me all the day,
I guess the boys felt sorry for me
because I was moving away.

GOD'S REUNION

In the barren hills of Golgotha
there was a crucifixion,
Prophecies of the Bible came true
and born was our religion.
At a desolate spot in those hills
the king of the Jews died,
As Roman soldiers gambled
and believers and the Mary's cried.

A huge stone was rolled in front
of His tomb that day,
It was almost humanly impossible
to move the stone away.
The morning after three days

He arose from His tomb of death.
Forty days He proved to all
He was the Son of God and then left.

Jesus said to His disciples,
"Witness for Me in our known lands—
like Jerusalem, Judea, and Samaria."
Then He raised high His hands—
instantly a cloud covered Him
and God took Him away,
And two angels of the Lord promised,
"That He'd return the same way."

At the foot of the cross
you must always strive to stay,
For any hour you might be lifted
up a Golden Pathway;
That leads to a great reunion
in Heaven one day,
The time is not determined yet
but it's not too far away.

HARP MAN

There was a music man
who had but one talent,
He played the harp beautifully
as though heaven sent.
He carried the harp with him
wherever he went,
Played it with perfection—
it always paid the rent.

He died suddenly
one Friday night late,
Soon faced St. Peter

at the Golden Gate.
St. Peter said, "It's a mistake,
we're filled with deep sorrow—
But you're not due to be here
until sometime tomorrow."

"Bring your harp back with you
and I'll know that you're the one,
Meanwhile, just go back
and have a night of fun."
So, back home he traveled
and once again he did go,
To a bar he often visited
called Sam Frank's Disco.

Almost all the night
he played his good old harp,
Beautiful melodies,
he had never been so sharp.
He danced, told jokes,
laughed until he cried,
Threw his harp in a corner
and smilingly died.

"Here I am St. Peter,
thanks for that one day treat!"
"But where is your harp?"
Asked dear old St. Pete.
At once the harp player
started to sing softly and low—

I left my harp

in Sam Frank's Disco.

WITCH MYRTLE

I got the idea when Myrtle Brown
walked near me on Sycamore Street,
She wore a black dress much too large
and so were the brogans on her feet.
Last spring when she was baptized
it was her last full water bath,
Minutes before I ever saw her
body odor zoomed across my path.

There was a great big wart
that protruded far out from her chin,
She called that black thing a dimple
but everyone knows a dimple turns in.
Mother Nature somehow hit Myrtle
in the face with a big ugly stick,
In a contest held to pick a town witch
Myrtle was a unanimous pick.

I didn't want her to be a girlfriend
I just came up with some dark-sided notion,
That concerned a sorcerer that could possibly
concoct me an "old age" potion.
I asked her, "If she could make such
an old age potion for a man like me?"
She answered, "I think it is possible
if you have a little gold we'll see."

Weeks later she gave me the potion
it was a clear rejuvenation oil,
I rubbed just a little on my body
and quickly my blood began to boil.
My muscles began to tighten and
my pale skin was now a golden beige,
I felt like a young man once more
the potion was working against old age.

Most of the many changes to my body
were ones that others could not see,
It was an inner feeling that my person
was changing so drastically.
When I gazed into any mirror
I looked better than I used to be,
But all the changes to my person
was what my imagination gave to me.

I kept feeling younger and younger
until my bottle of potion ran out,
I looked everywhere for Witch Brown
and her name I began to shout.
Finally she told me, "There has
never been an old age potion,
Your youthful appearance was
nothing but a gratifying notion."

Our imagination can really trick us
as I look at those days with a smile,
'Twas the most unforgettable moments
I've had in a long, long while.
When all is written in the Book of Life
you'll see on that final page,
That parents, health habits and God
makes the potion for old age.

CY

A hometown marine
by the name of "Cy,"
Went to war
like most other guys.
He lost a lot of friends
and his closest pal,
He lost his own eye—

on Guadalcanal.

A Japanese grenade
exploded close by,
Metal flew everywhere
hitting "Cy" in the eye.
At first doctors thought
that he might die,
But, he fooled them all—
for he was a tough guy.

They searched the hospital
and everywhere in town,
But there was no glass eye
that could ever be found.
They made an eye of oak—
a long-lasting wood,
Painted the pupil dark blue
and it looked pretty good.

They put the wooden-eye in
with a simple operation,
"Cy" spent many months
in lonely recuperation.
He became very self-conscious
and often would cry,
To make things even worse
they called him "Wooden-Eye."

Soon "Wooden-Eye"
became his nickname,
He knew that never again
would things be the same.
He would always regret
his "Wooden-Eye" fate,
Reluctantly he returned
back to his home state.

Books and radio
helped him stay at home,
But soon his loneliness
made him want to roam.
No matter how hard he tried
he'd often cry and shout,
And that sooner than later
he'd have to go out.

One night there was a dance
down at the YMCA,
"Cy" got up enough nerve
to venture that way.
He was very nervous
and close to tears,
Until he saw this girl
with great big ears.

He could ask her to dance
without any fear,
She couldn't kid about his eye
'cause she had big ears.
He asked, "Do you care to dance?"
"Wouldn't I!" Her answer was clear—
"Cy" in a mad voice said,
"Big ears! Big ears! Big ears!"

TO SEW OR NOT TO SEW

For some strange reason
which I will never know,
I picked up needle and thread
and began to sew.
For any man to even try
was very, very dumb,

I stuck the needle
deep into my thumb.

The blood dropped out
and hit the floor,
If only I had gotten
the thimble from the drawer.
That small puncture wound
taught me one thing for sure—
To leave sewing to women
'cause I ain't doing it anymore.

THE INTRUDER

Out in the garden I had been,
as I opened the door to enter in;
A big horsefly buzzed by my chin—
it dived and soared and did a tailspin.

Soon his hairy legs, so very thin,
landed on my glass of tonic and gin;
With no way to tell where he had been,
I got the fly swatter, and squashed him.

To some, I might've committed a mortal sin,
But to flies, a message I thought I would send—
"That intruders will never have the guts again,
to fly in my air space be he foe or friend."

JOE AND ME

Fellers just shake their heads
and think we're so dumb,
When we try to 'splain
where it is that we come from.

Our address down at the P.O.
is just 20 Plumb,
That is, 20 miles out
and plumb up a hollow at Crum.

Joe is a distant kin of mine
he's my pal and bestest "chum,"
Farm life gets us lonely and bored
and hankering for some fun.

Saturday we went to a beer joint
on Bull Creek called Lum's,
There's a lot of free lovin' going on
and we were aiming to get us some.

We drank warm beer all day
chased it with 'shine and dark rum,
We finished the night playing Black Jack
losing a pocket watch and a tidy sum.

We staggered out of the joint
when daylight was beginning to come,
We had the world's greatest hangover
and looked like a red-neck bum.

We walked 'til the sun had hit its zenith
and saw our shack at 20 Plumb,
Then Joe with a slurred voice said,
"Boy! I bet we had fun."

LISTEN

Hark! An inner voice calls
Like a spring song
Towards my heart it falls,
Telling me that all is wrong.

But I heed it not—
I did not listen
I soon forgot.

Hark! Again it calls at night
This time in a voice more clear,
It tells me I'm not doing right
I shut it off, I do not hear.
I heed it not—
I did not listen
I soon forgot.

Hark! The voice calls again
I know it is my soul,
And just like the wind—
I let it blow.
I heed it not—
I did not listen
I soon forgot.

Hark! I call you,
You must hear,
Listen whatever you do,
You have so much to fear—
The voice shook me thru and thru
But somehow I heeded it not—
I did not listen
I soon forgot.

Hark! And then a silence deep,
That touched me most of all—
I was lost and could not sleep,
Without my soul to call.
Regrettably, I heeded it not—
I wished I'd listened
But I forgot.

But, a mortal without a soul
Only down can be his fall,
Eternity can never be a goal—
Without a soul to call.
Never heed it not—
Listen to it carefully
It can not be forgot.

JOHN'S BOAT

John had a mighty fine
three-seated boat,
The only one around
that would still float.
Most of the time
he'd ride us for free,
But when he was broke
he charged a small fee.

He'd say, "Today there is
nary a free ride,
For a penny I'll take you
to the Kentucky side.
For three cents
I'll take you to the tipple,
And throw in a free ride
through those swift ripples.

And if you should have
lots of gosh-durn time,
You can ride all day
for one thin dime.
Or if you got some
company store script,
We'll travel down the Tug
to the rocks for a dip."

We searched every pocket
with both hands,
Found a knife, a penny
and a rubber band,
Also an old genuine
Indian throwing rock.
"That's good," said John
and he keyed the boat lock.

Too many of us got
into John's boat,
But with tin-can bailing
we stayed afloat.
For the longest time
we had so much fun.
Laughing and yelling,
and soaking up sun.

Floating down the rapids
water came over the sides,
Fear showed in all the faces
an emotion we couldn't hide.
John's boat sank quickly
and never could be found,
We all swam to shore safely—
just happy not to drown.

BELOW BELO

People that I meet-
always ask me "Son
where in this world
do you come from?"
Invariably I tell 'em
'Bout six miles from Crum.
If they ain't heard of that

65

then I know they're dumb.

I tell them, "I live west
of Naugatuck on Rt. 52,
Don't bat your eyes
when you pass through,
'Cause you will miss it
probably, if you do.
Stay in our town for awhile
It'll be good for you."

If they look at me funny
and still don't seem to know,
I tell them it's a hop, skip
and a jump below Belo.
In West Virginia's youngest county
that's called "bloody" Mingo.
Just follow the Tug River
and to our town you'll go.

When you stop in our town
and you are greeted with a hug,
And offered some "home-brew"
from an old brown jug;
And you see the youngin's
doing the jitterbug.
Then you are in Kermit—
the "gateway of the Tug."

THINGAMAJIG

It doesn't take an Einstein
that knows the art of Trig,
It doesn't take an Irishman
just to dance an Irish jig;
Any wind can blow a house down

66

why not ask the three little pigs,
But it does take great knowledge
to understand a thingamajig.

You can hear the word
no matter where you go,
Among the country folks
it's one they use and know.
Maybe it was a word of slang
discussed at the country store,
'Tis an expression word coined
in a place there ain't no more.

No matter what its meaning
there's such a daggone word,
In the rural lands of America
where often it can still be heard.
Wherever people might labor
you might hear one of them say,
"Hand me that thingamajig
'cause I need it right away."

A thingamajig could be a tool
we're not sure what kind,
It could be words imagined
or figments of the mind.
Is it a noun or pronoun?
An adjective or a verb?
It's in no English book to see
so, it might not be a word.

Old expression words not in the
dictionary makes little sense,
Grandpa's hand them down
that has a meaning so immense.
Examples are: I reckon dagnabit
that if I had a gosh-durn dime,

I'd borrow your thingamajig
and make things rhyme.

ROCKIN' AND CHURNIN'

Granny put another log on the fire
the room was already too hot,
She put a pillow in her rockin' chair
and patted it quite a lot.
She held me in her left arm
it was a secure but gentle lock,
She placed the butter plunger
into a two-tone brown crock.

As the fire reached its height
and its embers began to be burned,
She sat in her rockin' chair and
churned and rocked, and always churned.
Raising the lid slightly to see
if butter had formed atop the cream.
Granny rocked and churned, churned
and rocked for hours it seemed.

She got the milk from the ice box
it was in a tall light blue pitcher,
The butter was as smooth as silk
and no spread could ever be richer.
She kept it in a green "Duz" bowl
just waiting to be spread,
Upon her smoothly textured,
perfect, light brown, cornbread.

Granny could cook something
out of nothing that was superb,
She prepared the food with TLC
secret ingredients and garden herbs.

Eating in the "good old days"
was excellent, delicious and true,
The food was not store bought
but it was good and filling to you.

Now you can buy milk and butter
in just about any chain store,
Granny's old broken rocker
couldn't be repaired anymore.
Her old crock churn is shattered
and no one found a way to restore,
Her old grandfather clock chain
is rusted and can't chime as before.

In the good old days food was hard
to come by and there was no waste,
Most of those old folks wisely learned
that lots of time equals flavor and taste.
She churned, rocked and churned
a lot of patience on her face she wore,
I shall never forget my Granny
there's no one I could more adore.

PEACHES

She was all girl
anyone could see,
With big brown eyes
as dark as they could be.
She was sitting atop
a huge Sycamore tree,
When she came down
she tore her dungarees.

She wanted to play with us
in our tackle football game,

If we let this cute girl play
nothing would be the same.
We warned she might get hurt
she'd only have herself to blame,
For it was a hard-nosed contest
and sportsmanship was not an aim.

Harry ran the ball up the middle
and very hard she tackled him,
This time he ran to the left
and she tackled him again.
There was no one to block her
she was so fast and sly,
She made tackle after tackle
and didn't really seem to try.

Who was this girl that we
knew tackled very tough?
She had played the tackle game
before and became so rough.
What name should we call her?
Her peachy cheeks came to mind—
And from that day was called Peaches
a name that made her seem kind.

Peaches was always a lady
except on the football field.
And there she was an animal
seemed no pity she would feel.
She'd knock your block off
and leave you to lay—
If Peaches put four boys out,
she considered it a good day.

Peaches was talented lots of ways
besides the game of football,
She could run, jump, swim,

and competitively do them all.
When she attended high school
she still played all our games,
And was really proud to be
called a tomboy name.

Peaches could dance like
Ginger Rogers while a young girl,
She did the slow dance so
gracefully it was out of this world.
She was exciting to watch
as the floodwaters of the Tug,
But her best dance was with
Oscar or Jack, doing the jitterbug.

The last I heard of Peaches
she had settled down with Dan,
He was a perfect match for her
and was a kind and gentle man.
She is a religious woman now and
talks about the Heavenly scene,
And she's always been the best
looking tomboy I've ever seen.

HARRY CURRY

Do you remember
old man Harry Curry?
For a light green Buick
he traded his surrey.
Drove proudly thru town
but never in a hurry,
For he wasn't the type
to ever, ever, scurry.

An item Nora needed

from the commissary,
"I'll get it fast
just don't you worry.
It'll take some time
but I'll not hurry."
Those were the last words
heard from Harry Curry.

It was a snowy day
in the middle of January,
His Buick slid into the river—
didn't find him 'til February.
Carried his frail body
to the local mortuary,
With some deliberation
they wrote his obituary.

When spring came
and bloom was on the berry,
They carried at a snails pace
his body to the cemetery.
The ground had thawed
so they could finally bury,
And say their last goodbye
to old man Harry Curry.

The service was conducted
by Reverend Canterbury,
Who softly and slowly
read Harry's obituary.
A couple of lines summarized
the life of Harry Curry,
It simply said, "Except once,
Harry was never in a hurry."

OLD PORCH SWING

The hot day of summer was over
and the cool of the evening sat in,
Our good, meager supper was finished
and family leisure time was to begin.
With great anticipation for the evening
no one knew what the night would bring,
We hurried outside to the verandah
to sit in the old porch swing.

We might hear a homespun tall-tale
told by our funny Uncle "Duck,"
If Mary Brewer joined us and told
ghost stories—then we were in luck.
Aunt Ester spoke about all the gossip
and folks added other things,
As boards creaked and chains groaned
from the motion of the old porch swing.

Sometimes we had simple refreshments
like Kool Aid and popcorn,
And a big homemade molasses cookie
that would fill you up 'til morn.
And by the music of the Crosley radio
those that could, would try to sing,
We enjoyed the time spent together
sitting by or in the old porch swing.

Family closeness and values disappeared
with 'em the slow and easy life was gone,
Replaced by an age of speed, hurry
and the fast days of go and run.
If we'd return once more to the simple life
when we had only the basic things,
And wouldn't it be nice to ride again
in one of the remaining old porch swings.

DEEP WOODS HILL

I was born in a cabin
on Deep Woods Hill,
A spot so wonderfully
peaceful and still.
A place where your future
is of no fast worry,
A perfect area for the past
that was never in a hurry.

I miss Ma and Pa a lot
now that they've gone,
In a right direction
I've always tried to roam.
They watch over me from
the places where they rest,
They're on Deep Woods Hill
a few feet from the crest.

I miss the smell of Pa's pipe—
made of cobblestone,
And the "tabacca" he used
that was always home-grown.
I miss the taste of his 'shine
'twas the best I've ever known.
I miss the taste of Ma's cooking,
the soup beans and corn-pone.

That was a few recollections of
many years that had gone past,
And as the years rolled by
I realize they've moved too fast.
Lost to me was a way of life—
everything that really mattered—
Quickly eroded peacefulness
and a silence shattered.

With modern day conveniences
appearing all over this place,
It made my muscles shudder
and put a frown upon my face.
Lumber companies began to
"clear-cut" all the trees,
And bulldozers lined up to
strip coal with ease.

Now, as I grow older
I left Deep Woods Hill,
I've never been back
and I guess I never will.
From a distance I see
the damage they've done,
Like a fishless, muddy stream
and a dust-out of the sun.

There's supposed to be a law
to reclaim the coal-less land,
To plant flowers, and trees
and make the area look grand.
Why are guilty ones not fined?
No one has the slightest clue.
Most violators aren't bothered
they know what to do.

When I win the lottery,
and I know I soon will—
I'll make my land green again
in the valley and up on the hill.
Though the land will never,
never be the same until—
All bird and animals life return
to my Deep Woods Hill.

BRANCHO BRAVO

Clara had just had a boy
and couldn't think of a name,
She'd heard them all before
they were ordinarily the same.
She twirled a world globe
and when it began to slow,
Her finger landed on a place
called Brancho Bravo.

She thought it a proud name
and few had heard it before,
Her boy's name from thence on
became Brancho Bravo Moore.
His childhood days were good
and nothing unusual was in store,
Life on the farm was monotonous
and he was tired of doing chores.

At 16 he enlisted in the army
shortly before the Mexican War,
By the age of 22 he'd made Captain
and army life he began to adore.
Pancho Villa became real to him
and the ensuing battle wasn't folklore,
He knew lots of soldiers would die
in a battle he'd like to ignore.

From an overlooking mountain
he studied how to take this town,
Captain Bravo watched the enemy
thru binoculars as he looked down.
Then his artillery began to burst
causing terrible havoc all around,
Now he found himself leading
the troops up to this bloody ground.

He and his men ran fast into town
his sword was pointing high,
He did not have an inkling
that it was his time to die.
A single shot rang out
from an almost silent sky,
The brave Captain was hit
and put his hand upon his eye.

Falling he grabbed a sign post
that was implanted nearby,
Soon the battle was over
and again the birds began to fly.
The Captain gave his young life
at a place where no one goes,
'Twas ironic for the sign post read,
"Town of Brancho Bravo."

A PALLET ON THE FLOOR

Our house was a nice old house
and it was comfortably small,
There was always a big problem
when family came to call.
About as soon as they entered
through the homemade door,
Granny started gathering quilts
from the shift-robe drawer.

Time worn and tattered quilts
she tried very much to ignore,
But got her most beautiful ones
and left stacks of many more.
On top of the colorful linoleum—
recently bought at the store,
There was space for everyone

77

to have a pallet on the floor.

The pallets weren't as comfortable
as that newly built ritzy hotel,
But it would leave memories that
would be enjoyable to tell.
Memories that'll be lost otherwise
and probably never told anymore,
But I shall always remember Granny
making that pallet on the floor.

GRANDMA'S APRON

Grandma's aprons were made
from material of printed calico,
She sewed them from feed sacks
many long years ago.
Her aprons had so many uses
they're difficult to recall,
I remember a few of her apron uses
but I could never recollect them all.

The apron protected her dress
as she went about her many chores,
Sometimes her apron would be used
to dust the furniture and door.
And she'd use the edge of it
while wiping her Grandson's nose,
Often she would carry flowers in it
like peonies and the thorny rose.

In spring she'd use it as a basket
to hold her deep woods greens,
Along with ramps and mushrooms
as pretty as any ever seem.
In summer she'd harvest vegetables

and carry them in her apron sack,
Clothespins she carried in her apron
for the clothesline out back.

Today we only see fancy aprons
on a chef that is seen on TV,
Maybe a welder, at a butcher shop,
at your nicer restaurants or a bakery.
All of those aprons had a few uses
the owner might depend upon,
but none could compare to the uses
that Granny had for her apron.

BLACK TRUNK

Mom kept some sentimental
memorablia hidden away,
She kept 'em in an old black trunk
and looked at them on certain days.
Neatly wrapped in a colorful
flag of the rising sun,
Was a shiny banzai sword
and two rusty SKS handguns.

Beneath was a chain with dog tags
some rusted and some were bent,
Reminding her of the uselessness
of the war and possibly its intent.
There were many love letters
tied into a bow neatly,
Stating their love for each other
forever and completely.

There were stacks of pictures
from the islands where he had been,
It was easy to see my Dad

he was the one with the biggest grin.
Playing, laughing and posing
on some Pacific island shore,
Pictures of all the men ready to accept
whatever fate had in store.

Tears came to Mother's eyes
no matter how hard she tried,
Every time she saw that velvet box
with the Purple Heart inside.
She remembered those few short days
when she'd become his bride,
and he'd given his life for his country
and she accepted the fact with pride.

Years later, I was looking for something
and the attic ladder I pulled down,
I forgot what I wanted up there
but a lost memento I found.
Laying quite close to me
was a dusty old black trunk,
I quickly opened it and threw
out a lot of useless junk.

I kept my parent's picture at the
St. Valentine's Dance of Sweethearts,
They deeply loved each other even
back when they had their start.
She faithfully kept their marriage vows
never thinking about 'Til death do us part!
Until one day she was given posthumously
a velvet box with a Purple Heart.

THE WAKE

A terrible accident happened

at the #21 Holden coal mine,
It injured several good men but
it killed the best pal of mine.
The roof collapsed where Billy
was loading a car with coal,
Billy was a God-fearing man
and we didn't fear for his soul.

Billy laid in state at his home
in a casket of pine painted white,
Everyone that entered the room
held back tears with all their might.
A gold Bible lay in his crossed arms
over his suit that was dark blue,
The red tie and white shirt made him
appear not the Billy that we knew.

Billy usually wore a flannel shirt
and a pair of old faded jeans,
On his feet were hard toe boots
about as dirty as you've ever seen.
Goodbye letters and dozens of roses
were placed in the casket with him,
Roses were never his favorite flower
and letters he'd never read them.

All his friends were shocked that
he had died at such a young age,
His snuffed-out life was worth more
than his one dollar a day wage.
The next night they had his wake
up Marrowbone Creek Hollow,
There was Gospel preaching and
sad lonesome singing to follow.

During the wake about all the men
sat down on the darkened porch,

And drank from bottles of moonshine
'til their throat felt like a torch.
They talked mainly of poor old Billy
of both good times and the bad,
All remarked on several occasions
he was the best friend they ever had.

The women folk gathered by the table
they talked of Billy and his family,
Of his smiling face and youthful ways
and soon he'd be only a memory.
Some of them chatted, drank coffee,
ate homemade pies and cakes,
and with red eyes all were sad faced
as they said goodbye at Billy's wake.

The rooster crowed twice that dawning
over that foggy land so hilly,
We were leaving his sad wake but went
back to say our last goodbye to Billy.
John said, "All our bodies we don't own
they're a gift from God that's on loan,
So, be ready when your time's gone
and God calls you to come home."

SPARROW

As straight as an arrow
a tiny gray-brown sparrow,
Flew into my glass door
it would fly no more.

Feathers stuck with ease
blown gently by a breeze.
Its wrinkled claws clenched
and at times its chest winced.

Many morbid questions set in
as the sparrow's life came to end,
I asked, "Do birds have a soul?
Is there an eternal place to go?

Is there a lovely Heavenly meadow—
where good weather winds blow,
Where songs of birds constantly flow?"
I sure hope so, but only God knows.

When I go thru the gates of Heaven
I'll search for the Garden of Eden,
And on a branch of a tree I see
my little sparrow singing happily.

COME RIDE WITH ME

The Kingdom Come train
is waiting on the track,
It's waiting for you and
might not be coming back.
Angels will punch your ticket,
believers are welcome aboard.
There's a seat for everyone
the Great Engineer is the Lord.

If your life has been sinful
with despair, stress and strain,
If you're sick or forlorn
then board the Kingdom Come train.
There's nothing in the world to lose
but a restful eternal life to gain,
It's a place down the rails
with no tears, sorrow or pain.

The first stop is Heaven

where you'll see once again,
Hundreds of your forgotten
dearest and ageless friends.
In a special spot sits Mom,
Dad and all your nearest kin,
Some of them wouldn't be there
except God forgave their sin.

Hop on the train right now
it goes to Kingdom Come land,
Spend eternity in Heaven
where life is happy and grand.
Leave worldly things behind
wake from that sinful trance,
Come ride with your guardian angel
it could be your last chance.

OSCAR'S CAFÉ

Most memories fade
and will never last,
But one memory remains
from that long ago past.
It seems as vivid now
as it was that day,
When for the first time
I visited Oscar's Café.

Beside the cash register
smoking his big black cigar,
Talking in broken English
was our friend Oscar.
Oscar ran his Café
with an iron hand,
Took care of any trouble
as good as any man.

Virgil was by the jukebox
neat and clean shaven,
A crowd gathered by
as he quoted the Raven.
Virgil recited it eloquently
and punctuated it with a grin,
If the crowd applauded
he would quote it again.

To the sound of "Stardust"
"Toot" danced with Anna Pearl,
They danced so smoothly
as they did the "dip" and "twirl."
Then Jack and Anna Mary
began to dance the "jitterbug,"
To the music of Glen Miller
they really cut a rug.

The best of the evening
was Jack doing the "jitterbug,"
Fancy steps he had learned
in the valley of the Tug.
The night had gone fast
'twas time for me to depart,
I recorded all those memories
in my mind and in my heart.

Lost to time is Oscar's—
gone is our favorite night spot,
Only a few remnants remain
on a weed-infested plot.
As soon as you're able
visit that memorable lot,
Place a few special flowers
like—Forget-Me-Nots.

MISS RUBY

One of the nicest teachers
that there ever could be,
Was our 4th grade teacher
we all called "Miss Ruby."
She was a red-haired beauty
a heart-throb kind of gal,
She treated us firm and fair
and still somehow was our pal.

Later as seniors she taught sewing
of cotton fabrics, satin and silk,
While eating, she taught proper
etiquette and how to sip our milk.
Miss Ruby taught many things
be you a boy or be you a girl,
Things that could be used in life
as we met a cruel old world.

She taught the required things
while keeping us on the ball,
And implanted intangible particulars
that was on automatic recall.
She gave us the meaning of self worth
and to study deeply the things we saw,
But the most valuable info she taught
she wasn't supposed to teach at all.

She taught us respect for others
and to improve our morals and values,
We learned to be good citizens
and to ourselves always be true.
We became more tolerant of others
and to love the red, white, and blue,
All those fine attributes we learned,
Miss Ruby, we got them all from you.

Someday we will answer the call
of God and reach Jordan's shore,
We will visit Ruby at a Place
where she teaches once more.
There, a group of teachers listens
intently, under a shady sycamore—
As Ruby talks in her angelic voice
about learning and life as before.

HARRY ZINN

There once was a wealthy man named Harry Zinn
who had a hundred or more so-called friends.
Time passed and his wealth came to an abrupt end,
He thought that he'd stay with some so-called friends.
Much like a beggar he went to all of them,
they acted as if they had never known him.
For the next months life was just gin and an iniquity den,
he plotted ways to get even with his so-called friends.

Thanks to the lottery his wealth returned again.
And Harry never forgot the days when life was so thin.
He never forget how mean his so-called friends had been.
He returned home and managed to forgive all of them.
He looked in all the places where they should have been.
He searched everywhere in vain over and over again.
But there was no use because he could not find one friend.
The trail of each seemed to disappear around the bend.

Then a thought came to mind as his life began to end,
he could count on his fingers only friends less than ten.
Friends that he could count on through thick or thin,
Harry left this cruel world with just a few true-friends.
Harry went to Heaven and he knew that once again—
he'd be united with at least some friends, and kin.
If there is a moral to the poem, simply it must have been—

that one should be grateful for just a few true-friends.

COUNTRY COOKING

There is a restaurant
in these West Virginia hills-
If you are a hillbilly
and you need a good meal,
Come as you are
they certainly will fill—
That stomach of yours
over at Diehl's.

The atmosphere is charming
so relaxing and still,
Relics of the past
line their window sill.
If you want a place to eat
that is simply ideal,
Drive over to Nitro
and visit Diehl's.

On the everyday menu
you can choose any meal,
And the price is right
it's really a good deal.
Food that is so country
with flavor that's real,
Make sure you drive over
and check out Diehl's.

You would appreciate any
of their scrumptious meals,
Their baked steak is just right
and so is their veal.
The food's all homemade

and the potatoes they peel—
If it's home cooking you want,
go over to Diehl's.

The home-baked desserts
have that delicious appeal,
You'll be pleasantly surprised
when handed the bill.
It is such a bargain price
it's practically a steal,
At the greatest country kitchen
over at Diehl's.

INSIDE A TIRE

The bravery and courage
you just had to admire,
As the young boys rode
down a steep hill inside a tire.
A rolled up body almost
like a round ball,
They held on tightly
to the inside tire wall.

Never could you ever
equal that exciting thrill,
As you rode so fast
down sagebrush hill.
It seemed as though
you'd better have a Will,
Because it was possible
that the ride might kill.

When the tire began to
go around and around,
And you'd see the quickly

change of sky and ground.
And the occasional sun
outlining the sagebrush,
The excitement swelled
and made the adrenaline rush.

Then the tree impact came
it knocked all your air out,
You came out of the tire okay
but sure was bounced about.
You can, from ear to ear,
give out a big thankful grin,
Then promise that never
to ride inside the tire again.

If it were only possible
to see your old friends,
And you were young enough
to ride in a tire again.
You would do it once more—
but this could never be,
So you'll just cherish riding
the tire in memory.

POLLY McCOY

Wally was a good boy
and always went to school,
Some thought him a genius
but acted like a fool.
Wally's behavior was bad
he didn't want to learn,
Just scratched on a pad
and didn't give a gosh-durn.

Wally's mother's name

was Polly McCoy,
And like most mothers
she wanted a perfect boy.
Wally knew that his Mom
would cry and shout,
When the report cards
finally came out.

When Polly saw Wally's grades
she grew very, very mad,
She went to see all the
teachers that Wally had.
As she passed the classroom
she saw Wally doodling on a pad,
Not paying any attention
and his attitude seemed bad.

"Can my Wally learn?"
Polly asked Mrs. Dunn,
"Or is he playing games
and here only for the fun?"
Mrs. Dunn answered,
"From September until May,
I hate to tell you Polly—
Wally doodles all day."

ESCAPE

A few miles from Harmon
is a beautiful retreat,
A place so charming
where Heaven and nature meet.
A land where nature's hush
creeps across moss knee deep,
Beside green meadows so lush
with flowers until summer sleeps.

Where the call of the wild turkey
you can still hear,
And tracks are plain to see
of bear and deer.
Where a white pine tree
from a northerly tries to hide,
But its limbs are blown free
from the windward side.

It's a place where native trout
swim swiftly upstream,
Then quickly strikes out
through the water so green.
A sanctuary for birds
among the blueberries,
An asylum from words
and a slowness from hurry.

If you need to escape to a place
with a relaxing view,
Then take a long hike
through the hills to—
Where Heaven and nature meet
a place created by God,
There are no visions finer
than those found on Dolly Sod.

MAKING OUT

Kenny met Dolly
just by luck,
Got her to ride
in his new red truck.
In a short while
he pulled over to park,
Dolly said, "Not yet

wait 'til it's dark."

They went to a Xmas party
and danced until one,
Now it was time for
the parking fun.
As Kenny drove along
the wheel sounded loose,
The truck began to wobble
like a quivering goose.

Sparks flew everywhere
as hardtop met steel,
In the rear view mirror—
he saw his wheel on the hill.
Then Kenny sang to Dolly
in a voice high and shrill,

"You picked a fine time

to leave me loose wheel."

OLD JACK

There was a very smart
dog called "Old Jack."
He was the leader of
a well trained pack.
The dogs were various kinds
that numbered about 15,
They were the most organized
that anyone had seen.

The pack followed "Old Jack"
every single day,

Any rules made by Jack
they would always obey.
Whether it was time to eat
or just time to play,
Whatever they did
they did it Jack's way.

"Old Jack" taught his pack
proper sniffing lessons,
And a proper way to mount
so there would be no questions.
Also to cover with dirt
the place they'd been messing,
And when they passed a fireplug
which leg they should be lifting.

Old timers sitting at the depot
as they did almost every day,
All swore to these words
they heard "Old Jack" say,
"Fellas, back up against the curb
and strike a defensive pose,
'Cause coming up the street
is that dog called "Cold Nose."

SOUTH BRANCH

If my final days were near
and I had but one wish,
I'd love to return again to
the South Branch and fish.
To a spot where time
disappears without a trace,
Leaving unforgettable memories
that puts a smile on your face.

We drove towards Smoke Hole
just Richard, Ron and me,
Then up a mountain road
we traveled so anxiously.
Parked only a few feet
from the South Branch stream,
Went inside an old school bus
it was comfortable and clean.

Through the door we saw
a smiling Mayo at the table,
With a fifth of Old Crow
and a case of Black Label,
playing cards and poker chips.
A cigar he began to smoke
and long before he was thru,
we were all asleep and broke.

There is scenery in this valley
seldom seen by the human eye,
Like tall outcropping mountains
that appear to scrape the sky.
A blue Heaven where red hawks
dart and bald eagles fly,
In the valley far below
you might see a deer run by.

While on the path thru life
we have just a few true friends,
And it would be so wonderful
to gather with them again.
Along the South Branch where—
the waters run fast and deep,
And fish just one more time
before our final sleep.

RED SOX CURSE

The Red Sox just accomplished
an impossible dream,
It was not a feat of individuals
but of all 25 men on the team.

The moon was in total eclipse
in a dark and eerie sky,
The Sox swept the Cardinals
about as easy as eating pie.

The so called curse of the "Babe"
was reversed today,
As the Red Sox won the Series
in a most convincing way.

The Red Sox fans suffered thru
a curse, errors, bad luck and tears,
And finally won a World Series
after trying for 86 years.

We offer our congratulations to the Sox
for many exciting reasons,
And ask, "Can you ever repeat as champs
in any of the next seasons?"

BOOK OF LIFE

In Heaven the Book of Life
reveals our deeds from cradle to end.
Our acts are always inked in
by the stroke of an eternal pen.
In your waning consequential years
make your bad deeds a blanch dim.
And the good deeds illuminate brightly

as you prepare to meet Him.

"TY"

The gymnasium was packed
but it just wasn't our day,
We had many chances to win
but breaks did not go our way.
The score was forty to forty
with twenty seconds to go,
Our best player got hurt and
couldn't shoot his free throws.

He was taken to the clinic
he was carried out on a cot,
Coach had to pick a sub
to try and make the shots.
He asked, "Who can make one?"
He tried to look them in the eye—
But all heads were bent down
except for little man "Ty."

Then a trembling hand was lifted
it shot high up into the sky,
"I'm sure I can make one, Coach,"
"Ty's" uneven voice made the reply.
"Okay "Ty " it is now your job,"
Coach knew he'd give it a good try.
The crowd grew deathly quiet
as the time to shoot drew nigh.

"Ty" toed close to the foul line
and took his deepest sigh,
Knew that the shot had missed
as soon as he let it fly.
His first shot was too hard

and hit the back of the rim,
The ball landed like a brick
when it came back to him.

He had only one more shot
and the situation grew grim,
Confident he could make it
though chances seemed slim.
"Ty" bounced the ball twice
and bent his shaky knees,
The ball went through the net
as "Pretty as you please."

Pandemonium quickly broke out
everywhere in those stands,
And the school song rang out
from Tommy's pep band.
Students laughed and smiled
but all yelled a repeated cry,
For their newest hero
"Ty!" "Ty!" "Ty!"

"RATTLETRAP"

I got me a 1940 Fairlane Ford
everyone called it a "rattletrap,"
Its outside had many kinds of paint
and its inside smelled like crap.
The motor looked almost new
it sounded like a purr from a kitten,
It was in perfect timing
and not one cylinder was missing.

I couldn't afford to run the Ford
'cause gas was so darn high,
When it shot up to 25 cents per gallon

all gas stations I passed by.
But sometimes my old "rattletrap"
quit purring and chugged instead,
Knowing that it was out of gas
to the nearest station I'd head.

One day I picked up this girl
she lived in Flat Gap,
I got us 2 gallon jugs of beer
it was good tasting tap.
But for all my trouble
all I got was a hard slap,
Still, parking was great fun
in my old "rattletrap."

My "rattletrap" days ended
many long years ago,
And now I drive a dent and
scratch-free silver Volvo.
It really belongs to the bank
and I expect it will never be mine,
No car has belonged to me
since back in my "rattletrap" time.

BOB

Among the beautiful long needled pines,
they lay to rest a good friend of mine.
Whispers from the visitors I began to hear,
as I placed by the flowers a six pack of beer.
With some time to pass I looked at headstones,
an hour passed until Bob and I were left alone.
A tear ran down my cheek and a chill thru my bone,
'til one bottle opened and soon the beer was gone.

As I slowly drove by the caretaker's home,

I heard an eerie ring from his outside phone.
I ran to the phone booth and put the phone to my ear,
and at once Bob's voice I could clearly hear.
He said, "We have about everything up here—
except the sin items like tobacco and beer,
But now I don't have time for idle chit-chat—
thanks for the beer pal for I sure needed that."

GRANDMA PATRICK

Father Time picked my pocket
of all the things so dear,
Mother Nature's mood went by
all those wonderful years.
Life has been so good to me
it matters not that I grow old,
Recently my Grandmother left me
and joined the Heavenly fold.

She left me beautiful memories
that no one can take away,
And they will linger in my mind
until that Judgment Day.
Those memories will then change
from mind-felt to real,
And my soul will soar with hers
high above the hills.

HOMELESS

I'm too proud to beg and too honest to steal,
Always in poor health and feel very ill.
I no longer even try; I don't have the will,
Cruel life has made me swallow a bitter pill.
I live on the streets in a house of cardboard,

Lately, a really good meal I cannot afford.
I wear old clothes they gave me at the YMCA.
I pray every night but I make no headway.

My voice cries to escape from this life of disgrace,
I know that my heart has been in the right place.
Someday my soul will drift to a place unknown,
But now I barely survive and I'm always alone.
I dream of the good life but it would be my guess,
That as the New Year approaches I'll still be homeless.
I can't understand how I ever got in such a mess,
Or how I ever drifted into this nothing-less abyss.

I wait each year for Thanksgiving and Christmas Day,
to eat their delicious and free dinner down at the YMCA.
I'll get turkey and trimmings and dessert on my tray,
I just hope and pray that each day could be a holiday.

3 MUSKETEERS

When I was a young lad
about the only candy I ever had,
Was made in Granny's kitchen
there was never a recipe to mention.
On a winter night she'd make it
sugar, cream and cocoa she'd mix it,
On a pot-bellied stove she'd boil it
'til it became shiny and she'd beat it.

Her process is still in my mind
I could see it now even if I was blind,
She repeated that way time after time
'twas a treat and didn't cost a dime.
Once I was playing by the old bank
saw a "V" nickel in the dark and dank,
Picked it up and rubbed 'til it began to shine

'twould buy a new candy bar all mine.

It was for a Musketeer bar it would pay
it was a nice 3 for 1 deal and it really made my day,
My taste was on high when I went to the café.
I ate one of its delicious parts right away.
I would save the rest for later that day
until a bully took a big bite and offered no pay,
I was mad for not putting up a fight
but two thirds of a Musketeer was all right.

My sweet tooth was not satisfied and I wanted more,
I pitched pennies at the Company Store.
It took hours but I won 5 pennies that day,
all the Musketeers were sold so I got a Milky Way.
There's a lot of difference in candy bars
especially those made by a company called Mars,
To experts and me, the best candy bar is very clear
#1 of all the bars was the 3 Musketeer.

TOWN SOUNDS

Remembering a nice sound
heard around our town,
Like crickets on the wind
whistles around the bend.
Calls of the whippoorwill
cowbells form orchard hill,
Empties heading for the tipple
and splashing of Tug ripples.

The clickety-clack of a train
the thunder before a rain,
The loud curfew siren
a beer-joint fighting scene.
Humming motors of cars

the jukebox at Oscar's.
Beat of the pumping station
steam from a train escaping.

Work on the N and W track
barking dogs in a pack,
Cussing by old man Gobe
tall tales spun by Tobe.
Bluegrass by Flatts and Scruggs
moonshine slushing in a jug,
"Dee" taking drunks to jail
a soft melodic church bell.
And then a silence fell.

D-DAY

Forget us not, when we are gone,
write nothing special upon our stone.
We traveled so far from freedom's home,
to show that injustice is not condoned.

We died on the beach midst sea and foam,
we died as we scaled those cliffs of stone.
We died that day and lay unknown,
we felt their pain and heard their groans.

We invaded Normandy 'cause freemen had to atone,
and the seeds of democracy had to be sown.
Good must vanquish evil; the Nazis had to be shown,
for freedom and liberties banner must be flown.

Now our spirits are at rest but they still roam,
they soar above Normandy by a free breeze blown.
Whispering, "Forget us not when we are gone,
write nothing special upon our stone."

I LOVE TO FISH

I like to fish for bass
in the Greenbrier's water of blue,
I like to fish for carp in the Tug
where the sewer empties thru.
But I love to fish on Twelve Pole
where I'm free to jump and shout,
In front of my good buddies
when I pull out a big trout.

SKIPPING ROCKS

Rocks found on a sandbar
are usually just a few,
Round rocks, flat rocks,
and thin ones too.
Round rocks won't skip—
make the sound of "kerplink,"
And splash the water
as they're thrown in and sink.

Flat and thin rocks are light
they will not travel far,
You'll be lucky if they land
ten yards from the bar.
The best skipping rocks can't
be located in any book,
But are quickly gathered
if you know where to look.

Boys know it's not the rocks
nor the distance you can throw,
But magic words and secrets
of a ritual you must know.
If you wiggle your nose and put

chew tobacco on your fingertips,
Then sidearm any rock and
like magic it'll—Skip! Skip! Skip!

SNOW CREAM

In those pollution free days
of winter very long ago,
My Grandmother would
often trek through the snow.
And find the perfect place—
to fill up her two bowls,
We always watched from a
spot at the large window.

In the kitchen she'd press
the crystal white snow down,
Into it she put lots of sugar
and swirled vanilla around.
She stirred in yellow cream
with an old wooden spoon,
Dished it out quickly to us
and it was gone so soon.

It would be impossible
to make snow cream today,
'Cause Granny is not around
to show us her special way.
There's no unpolluted snow
and condensed is the cream,
Now days, old time snow cream
can't exist, except in dreams.

SCRAPBOOK OF YOUR SOUL

A record of the days you've lived

is in the Scrapbook of Your Soul,
You have inscribed them in your
Book of Life and really didn't know.
You've painted pictures of beautiful days
and of times of worry and woe,
There's a table of contents of friends
and a very short list of foes.

You put in a long list of sinful deeds
that out number the ones that glow,
Nothing hidden, but all is scripted in the
Book of Life that you and God know.
There are devices that constantly records
and plays back any deeds by you,
God holds you liable for those actions
no matter what else you may do.

If that old Scrapbook of Your Soul
was placed in front of you,
Would you erase youthful errors
or obliterate what was new?
The soul is an unexplainable entity that flees
a physical being during its last breath,
It may wander in space for awhile but one day
will join the body from which it left.

Perhaps you've forgotten so many little sins
that has been written in indelible charcoal,
Ask forgiveness for all, confess your sins again,
and God will erase them from His scroll.
Before the Angel of Death comes calling you
pray that your name is on His final roll,
God judges by writings in the Book of Life
and from the Scrapbook of Your Soul.

NEW YEAR 2005

Almost all the decorations of Christmas
had been taken down,
Nowhere in the Heavens could the Star
of Bethlehem be found.
At 12:00 the old year left and quickly
came in the New Year of 2005,
A solemn night turned excitedly alive
much like a disturbed beehive.

There were celebrations, parties, dances,
and "kissie-wissies" galore,
Many New Year resolutions were made
and doomed to failure as before.
Almighty God should always have a hand
in any resolution plan,
Because our Savior would be successful
while no ordinary person can.

God could resolve so many things like:
famine, war, and an AIDS attack,
Freedom and democracy could exist
in the war-torn country of Iraq.
Moslem, Jew, and all people of the world
could reach a peaceful accord,
If during this New Year they'd turn
all disputes over to the Lord.

KERMIT

I've something to say if you'll permit,
about a place I know and can never forget.
A place that has always been my favorite hit,
it's my hometown of wonderful Kermit.

Sometimes when I'm blue and feel so all alone,
I think of the words, "There's no place like home."
I feel a tear suddenly come to my eye,
I always will "'til the day that I die."

For a mining town it was clean and neat,
with well kept homes and tree-lined streets.
Seemed much larger then, than it does now,
as we grow older things change somehow.

We had the most wonderful folks you could ever find,
so friendly and considerate, so gentle and kind.
They always guided us in the right direction,
they gave us their love and their affection.

They had certain beliefs that were heart-felt,
some honored J.L. Lewis and worshipped Roosevelt.
Some thought Hoover was a despicable knave,
took their convictions with 'em to the grave.

In Heaven, I think, that there could be found,
a peaceful little place like our hometown.
Just head straight for it, you need no permit,
"for it's almost Heaven" in the Town of Kermit.

FLU SEASON

Years ago there was a flu epidemic
that visited many American towns,
It made many people ill
and really put them down.
A lot of them died
and was cemetery bound,
Americans by the hundreds
were buried in hallowed ground.

It took years for the development
of a safe vaccine we knew,
That'd be effective against certain
strains of the most deadly flu.
Soon millions of shots were given
to people like me and you,
And a feeling of a healthy security
against our deadly flu grew.

Present vaccines were contaminated
with no time to make a new debut,
Fear and anxiety spread thru the elderly
and a felling of doom and gloom grew.
A lot of ordinary people asked,
"So what is new?
What in this old world
can millions of the elderly do?"

We stood in long lines for hours
and as the lines got shorter with only a few,
A sign pops up and reads
"We are closing for our day is thru."
A lot of the elderly complained
and were sick at their stomachs too,
All this happened 'cause the government
didn't make enough vaccine for the flu.

SWITCH

At Granny's house we had certain rules
that we followed to a "T,"
And if we happened to break one of them
there'd be a "switching" shortly.
It did not matter to her why, when,
or which child it was to be,
She striped our legs with a switch

'twas good-behavior therapy.

Her switch was on the mantle—
it was slender and long,
She seldom ever broke it—
it was extremely strong.
Granny swung the switch hard
it made a whistling crack,
It made tears run from our eyes
and stripes upon our back.

Often she would make us pull
a limb from an apple tree,
We had to stand erect and still
to take our hot "switch tea."
It taught us valuable lessons
that we could never see,
As we traveled down life's highway
the road was easy as could be.

Some folks would certainly hit the roof
if someone switched a child today,
"It'd cause mental and physical harm,"
at least that's what they'd say.
If it were only possible for someone
to switch with a loving smile,
Would it solve bad-behavior problems
or just ease them for awhile?

Modern day punishment for children
is meted out in so many ways,
They are given quiet time and grounding
and privileges taken away.
Most of her offspring are excellent citizens
and have carved out a worthwhile niche,
We know that our success is due to Granny
and that big long switch.

BELSPRING CHURCH

In the rolling hills of Virginia
near the peaceful water of the New,
Sits a church in a green valley
with such a picturesque view.
It's a beautiful country church
as white as flakes of snow,
With colorful stained-glass windows
that reflect a spectrum glow.

Members, guests, and families arrive
they are welcomed at the door,
With love, kindness, and sincerity
you just don't see anymore.
Handshakes, hugs, and smiles
and a bit of small-talk abound,
Before the Homecoming sermon
and dinner on-the-ground.

The choir of the Old Brick Church
stood up and began to sing,
The minister welcomed everyone
to the church at Belspring.
So, if you are close to Radford
on the third Sunday of July,
Visit our little country church
don't let the chance pass by.

BACKWATER BOB

A brave decorated hero
of the war in Vietnam,
When he fought the "Cong"
he learned not to give a damn.
He had no kind of job

nothing of value to own,
All he wanted from life
was to be left alone.

'Twas in the backwater area
that he built his lean-to,
He was too close to the river
maybe he didn't mean to.
His place was tarp covered
with a lot of cardboard,
His bed was a sleeping bag
it was all he could afford.

The state owned the land
and knew nothing of him,
Then some busy-bodies told
'cause he wasn't like them.
He's against the establishment
and the way they played the game,
Vietnam was not a proud war
the government was to blame.

About a mile or so upstream
grew large breaks of cane,
Among the similar looking plants
he grew his "Mary Jane."
Smoking a joint or two
relaxed his emotional strain,
He knew that it hurt his body
and at times affected his brain.

Monthly he went to the Post Office
when he got his disability check,
He came thru town with a war-bonnet
on his head and beads around his neck.
The days turned into months
and the months turned into years.

Sometimes his loneliness
made him shed a lot of tears.

His health began to deteriorate
and it became crystal clear,
That life had become so fragile
and his end was really near.
Over the emergency scanner
I heard the paramedic say,
"That sometime during the night
Backwater Bob had passed away."

The red lights of the ambulance
glared through that rainy night,
In the gurney was a black bag
that held a body out of sight.
They gave him a military funeral
one befitting a war hero,
Burial was in Arlington Cemetery
by some buddies he used to know.

Few remember Backwater Bob
he was a great and gentle guy,
He fought for his country
but he didn't know exactly why?

WASH TUB

The fire in the grate
was extremely hot,
It bought the temperature up
of the room quite a lot.
During the cool months
of September through May,
I was required to bathe by the fire
every single Saturday.

I put in the tub two buckets
of water from the well,
And all the boiling water
from a two-gallon pail.
The water soon mixed together
and was barely tepid,
My stay in the tub was too long
and the room became frigid.

It took a long time for water to be
put in the houses in our town,
Workmen buried many feet of water-
carrying pipes underground.
I could hardly wait for the plumbers
they worked for over an hour,
I hated that old galvanized tub
but I really loved our new shower.

A MILLION STITCHES

It was early in the morning
every couple of days or so,
Some ladies met at our house
they had come to sew.
Each carried a sewing basket
filled with materials and rags,
And leftovers from breakfast
in a rolled up paper bag.

The ladies worked on the quilt
until it was at least noon,
Some ladies left but some
stayed 'til late afternoon.
At times it was hard to see
the nails on the quilting rack,
And harder to get the cloth over

the tiny nails or small tacks.

But this rack folded up
made of oak and strongly built,
Strong enough to hold their
creation of a butterfly quilt.
Days of pattern patching
'til colors began to merge,
Into a cocoon and then
a butterfly quilt emerged.

When the fire died down
as it did on a cold night,
Jack Frost would reach thru the
windows to take a bite.
The house always got colder
'cause of porous and rough wood,
Though kicked off earlier
a quilt always felt so good.

Granny asked, "Ladies, what would
you wish if you could have two wishes?"
Ada answered, "To always quilt and to
get someone to wash the dishes."
Sara replied, "To always quilt
and Sam not to dig those ditches."
Jan lastly said, "I wish we'd always quilt
and make a million stitches."

BELLING

When I was a young boy
growing up in my hometown,
Every so often there would be
a belling coming down.
A few days after a couple

had "tied the knot,"
A gang gathered at night
usually quite a lot.

It was an Irish custom
that had been handed down,
Young and old folks alike
came from all over town.
Noisemakers included screams
and pounding on pots and pans,
Anything that made a noise
someone had in their hands.

The couple had married
only a few days ago,
A gang would gather
quietly at their window.
And in the quietness
of the darkest night,
Start belling with a noise-
maker with all their might.

We borrowed the wheelbarrow
out of the Shoemaker barn,
Whether it was returned or not
no one gave a darn.
We needed a wooden rail
and tore it from Jim's fence,
Why we actually needed both
did not make much sense?

As all the loud noise began
it awakened everybody around,
In a few minutes the bride was in
the wheelbarrow riding thru town.
And the groom was riding the rail
with a "butt" that was swelling,

We had a lot of laughs that night
'cause we had fun at the belling.

Later we entered the beer joint
where a "set-up" was in order,
The groom had to buy cokes for
the young and beers for the older.
As I think back to the humble
times of those good old days,
I remember all the great events
we enjoyed in such a simple way.

SPUTNIK

By a huge Russian rocket
an artificial satellite was hurled,
Out of the pull of gravity
across the Heavens it twirled.
Its orbit was an elliptical one
as it journeyed far from this world,
Little did anyone realize then—
that the Space Age was unfurled.

Every 98 minutes its orbit
took it to over our western sky,
It had a blinking red light
easy to see with the naked eye.
The year was 1952
a time that deserves a mention,
'Cause 'twas something that
instantly got the world's attention.

American technology had been
dealt a very decisive blow,
The Russian military might was more
accomplished than we'd ever know.

From that time on, each country
tried to out do the other in space,
To let an adversary excel militarily
could be a disastrous disgrace.

ICBMs were being tested
on USSR steppes and USA sand dunes,
Suddenly the world powers were
in a space race that wouldn't end soon.
For awhile Russia was far ahead
but quickly we changed that tune—
Because soon we heard an unlikely song
that we had landed on the moon.

After a few more trips to the moon
our interests in space began to decline,
Then, there's a lack of money, budget cuts
and a bad economy helped change our mind.
Made us cut deeply our space program
that'd been ongoing for such a long time,
At last the space race was ending
the costliest in the history of mankind.

Thanks to Putin and Bush relations
between the powers are on the mend,
Had it not been for Gorbachev
and Reagan being two futuristic men.
But if Sputnik had not orbited
around the earth away back then,
Who but God would ever know
what might have been.

POTOMAC KAYAKING

I had dreamed about it since '74
and in my mind it became a goal,

As soon as I saw the South Branch
and fished in its deepest holes.
For reasons unknown to me
I wanted to ride in a kayak,
Through the white waters of the
South Branch of the Potomac.

Pitching my old army tent about
the same place as before,
I heard the torrid river as its
water lapped the shore.
I was about to accomplish a
dream which I had prayed for,
Night came and I slept
waiting on my happy chore.

My head was wide-awake
when my feet hit the floor,
My hands held so many things
it was hard to shut the door.
Close to the old swinging bridge
I easily put the kayak in,
Slow was the lifeless current
as my venture was to begin.

In moments the river was violent
I paddled as hard as could be,
Peacefulness to turbulence
and now it was up to me.
The large whitecaps tossed
me about, to and fro,
And sent me in directions
I didn't want to go.

Paddling hard left, then right
I kissed off a large boulder,
My body was tense and tired and

so was my arm and shoulder.
At last I saw my destination
so near but yet so far,
And the spot where I
had left the hauling car.

I heard the repeating sound of
Slush! Slush! Slush!
And the endless waves making a
Swosh! Swosh! Swosh!
Then indecisiveness enveloped me
a Qualm! Qualm! Qualm!
My adrenaline rush was over and a
Calm! Calm! Calm!

Just one more big boulder
that I had to navigate by,
Like taking candy from a baby
or as easy as eating apple pie.
The kayak went thru a great wave
and the stream spit into my eye,
It was a way the river had of
showing I'd made a nice try.

Then I glided along in a
peaceful and serene stream,
And realized that this day
I had accomplished my dream.
I threw the river a kiss
and waved a reluctant goodbye,
I vowed to kayak the river again
one more time before I die.